The Shirburnian Catastrophe

Basil Diki

Langaa Research & Publishing CIG
Mankon, Bamenda

Publisher:
Langaa RPCIG
Langaa Research & Publishing Common Initiative Group
P.O. Box 902 Mankon
Bamenda
North West Region
Cameroon
Langaagrp@gmail.com
www.langaa-rpcig.net

Distributed in and outside N. America by African Books Collective
orders@africanbookscollective.com
www.africanbookcollective.com

ISBN: 9956-791-13-X

Table of Contents

Book I

Squaring A Circle

For Divine Warrior (DWD)
Born at dawn in July, 2013
Friend and son, welcome.
yn;\w&a[yn=B%t!yM*T^m=k*T!yB~w^T!yX@b[yn=l*p~
.<oul*l=
Ps 41:13

Let us not dream that reason can ever be popular. Passions,
emotions, may be made popular, but reason remains the
property of the few.

Johann Wolfgang von Goethe
German poet, 1749 - 1832

Characters

King Lima III, *King of Ngoloi (±45 yrs)*
Queen Mother Jirimita, *The King's Mother*
Queen Tiafora, *The King's 8th Wife*
Queen Amina, *The King's 10th Wife*
Queen Liliosa, *The King's 11th Wife*
Queen Ayola, *The King's 13th Wife (±17 yrs)*
Prof Pitoni, *A Royal Political Advisor*
Chuchu, *A Royal Diviner (Sangoma, Female)*
Radimir Ivanov *(White), A Royal Butler (±48yrs)*
Jefferson Buckley *(White), A Henchman (40s)*
Jervaulx Olowolagba *(Dwarf), A Royal Orderly*
PM Ete Gamato, *Prime Minister*
Katomene Hasa, *An MP (Early 40s)*
Belemina, *Katomene's Wife*
Mimudeh, *Katomene's Daughter (16 yrs)*
Archer McLeod *(White), Mimudeh's Boyfriend (18 yrs)*
Raj Gopal *(Indian), Queen Tiafora's Boyfriend*
Gen. Okata Ofuji, *An army Commander-General*
Royal Poet
Opposition President
Taji, *An Opposition Member (Executive)*

Plus:

A Scrum of Foreign Journalists Including:
-An American White Male (CNN)
-An Arabic Male (Al Jazeera)
-A British White Female (BBC)
-A Chinese Female (Xinhua)
-A Russian Female (Russia Today)

10 Executive Party Members *(Incl. a few Whites)*
A **Muscular Bodyguard**
A **Striptease Dancer** *(White)*
12 Members of a School Bagpipe Band
4 Supreme Court Judges
±10 High School Students *(Multi-Racial)*
An **Executive Partying Crowd**

Act One

Scene One

Midday
A palatial portico

GEN. OKATA OFUJI, *in a decorated ceremonial uniform complete with a holstered sword, is set to take an oath before* KING LIMA III *who is on his feet. The King is in a cowry headband, beads, an ethnic batik cloth and sandals. Between the King and the general are copies of the Holy Bible and Al Koran on an ornamental table. Behind the King is a grandiose armchair on whose backrest is the skin of a leopard. Seated in a row to the King's right are four robed and wigged Supreme Court Judges, to his left, standing, are* PM GAMATO *and* OLOWOLAGBA, *the dwarf, both in executive suits. On a reed mat in a corner is* QUEEN MOTHER JIRIMITA, *in lavish attire, and* CHUCHU, *a very old royal diviner. Bagpipe music is playing off-stage.*

The general touches the Holy Bible and Al Koran, salutes and brings the hand to rest on his chest. OLOWOLAGBA *steps forward and holds up a printed oath on a clipboard for the general to read.*

GEN. OFUJI
(*Reading*) **This day the third of September, I, Gen. Okata Ofuji, Commander-General of the Royal Defence Forces of Ngoloi, soberly, solemnly and within all my faculties, hereby swear my total allegiance to His Majesty King Lima III. Sir, I pledge to secure the King and the sacred Lima dynasty expeditiously, and to defend the territorial integrity and sovereignty of this your kingdom. Throughout my tenure as the**

5

Commander-General, and beyond, I shall be bound by the Royal Act, the Military Act and the Official Secrets Act whose breaching may be punishable by death. So help me God.

OLOWOLAGBA *lowers the clipboard and retreats. The general salutes again and shakes hands with the King across the table. The King's mother, rising, shrieks in continuous ululation and dances jubilantly on the mat, but* CHUCHU *remains seated, tacit. The judges rise, bow in unison and remain thus. Enter the* ROYAL POET, *holding a knobkerrie in his right hand and in his left a skin-shield and a spear. He raises the knobkerrie, a cue that halts the ululation, and launches into a performance.*

ROYAL POET
(*Reciting as he performs*)
Though I always say I am inferior clay,
Get ready to behold an invincible ray.
This glorious red-ochre day,
Young and old, near and yonder, lend ear.
Of gamma and infra-red aim we hear.
But darkness utter, he shattered!

The QUEEN MOTHER *ululates, but briefly this time.*

O, scatter, detractors, scatter!
Viva the bearer of the sacred spear!
Shiver at the voracious adder!
What is his eye but ancestral radar?

Outside, a whistle blows and a militaristic voice bellows an order.

MALE VOICE (OFF-STAGE**)**

Twenty-one gun salute! Gunners one to seven! Ready! (*Pauses*) Fire!!!

A singular, massive, thunderous gunfire sounds off-stage and smoke bellows into the portico from one side.

MALE VOICE (OFF-STAGE**)**

Gunners eight to fourteen! Ready! (*Pauses*) Fire!!!

A second gunfire roars off-stage followed by another offering of smoky plumes, which causes some judges and the Prime Minister to cough.

MALE VOICE (OFF-STAGE**)**

Gunners fifteen to twenty-one! Ready! (*Pauses*) Fire!!!

The gunfire roars off-stage for the third time, accompanied by the plumes.

ROYAL POET

(*Resumes performing*)
Black mamba, bear the kingdom yonder.
Giant in tradition and wisdom,
Doom detractors, African panda.
This sacred red-ochre day,
The Reed Dance honours you with a maiden,
To conduit your sacred seed into the Lion's den.
(*Bows repeatedly towards the King*)

Off-stage, the music's tempo and volume increase. The QUEEN MOTHER *resumes ululating as* MIMUDEH HASA, *mace-bearing in a fluffy, red, towering conical headgear strapped under her chin, leads a twelve-member multi-racial school band, all in black bonnets, playing the Scottish music. The drum major conducts the elegantly-dressed band onto the portico, and performs with childish resignation as flutes, drums and percussion mingle harmoniously.*

Curtain

Scene Two

Afternoon of same day
A cubicle in an ice-cream parlour

[Act 1]

MIMUDEH, *still in her bagpipe drum-major's uniform, and* ARCHER McLEOD, *in swanky wear, a digital camera lolling around his neck, are enjoying ice-cream at a table by a window. The schoolgirl's mace and red headgear are on the table. Voices of other teenage patrons in the same building can be heard laughing and commenting as they play snooker, darts and other games.*

MIMUDEH
How goes it so far, *Amigo?*

ARCHER
Bittersweet, girlfriend, though it's Tuesday and a holiday. The sweetness comes from your company; the bitterness from an anxiety to go back home and read, read, read. And don't call me *Amigo*.

MIMUDEH
(*Stubbornly*) It beats me, *Amigo*. Tell me, *Amigo*, why can't I call you *Amigo?*

ARCHER
(*Proudly*) Only my father and I call each other that, especially at the shooting club. But Mom goes haywire when I call him *Amigo*. She wants me to call him *Sir*, or Engineer

McLeod, as if I am his subordinate at the airport. Anyway, I am glad my dad is not a *mister*.

MIMUDEH

Neither is mine, boy. But at our crib no one calls him *honourable*. My parents are on a first name basis – Katomene, Belemina. (*Shrugs forlornly*) Since you won't ask, I'll tell you. I spent the morning at the royal palace. The occasion was an allegiance ceremony featuring the Commander-General.

ARCHER

(*Points at the mace and the headgear*) You were entertaining the Lion, instead of the predator amusing you. I wish you could take a cue from a circus. (*Shrugs forlornly*) In the morning my dad and I went to the shooting club. Now I can hit the bull's eye five out of six times. In the evening we'll attend a service at the Presbyterian Church. (*Sombrely*) We are considering a return to the cathedral. My mother – the Presbyterian – has caused us enough experimentation. We miss Father Tito's sermons and heavenly voice.

MIMUDEH

That has been your rhapsody for the last twelve months. (*Shrugs*) Are you going to offer a Presbyterian prayer for me in the evening?

ARCHER

I'll beg the Comptroller to keep you pure in flesh and in spirit. I'll ask Him to help you pass O-Level with distinctions. Isn't that delicious?

MIMUDEH

Tell me something *more* scrumptious, Archer — something that would halt the sun.

ARCHER

What could be more enchanting than my love for you? Promise me something, Mimudeh.

MIMUDEH

(*In mock annoyance*) Promises and promises, what must I promise?

ARCHER

Swear that I won't lose you no matter what happens. Swear, Mimudeh.

MIMUDEH

(*Laughs*) What if a tsunami happens, or Pyongyang and Seoul ignite the Third World War?

ARCHER

Stop kidding and stop prophesying war. I am damn serious, girlfriend.

MIMUDEH

But you are the one who is supposed to be making that promise.

ARCHER

Whoa! Whoa! Whoa! What are you driving at, girlfriend?

MIMUDEH

Next year you'll be at a medical school —abroad, I guess. University guys ditch their high school flames. I foresee you finding me embarrassing.

ARCHER

What would make me dump a spectacle like you? (*Thespian*) Where would I find an ornate rubbish bin to put a gem like you? If I lost you, I would lose my bearings forever. Yemudeh could be a cute proxy, if only she talked like you, laughed like you, smiled like you.

MIMUDEH

You always say that. It's so *flattering* coming from one Dr Archer McLeod who can't distinguish me from my twin. But do you really mean it?

ARCHER

Of course, but you must keep on excelling in your exams.

MIMUDEH

Though you are in the Sixth Form you might fail to go to university if you flunked your exams. (*Holds his hand*) My mother calls you Dr McLeod when the honourable isn't around. She's very fond of you and assures me you'll make it.

ARCHER *blushes.* MIMUDEH *picks the mace, rises and poses clownishly for him. He smiles, rises too and begins snapping her from different angles. Outside, motorcade sirens blare, booming. The off-stage voices in the building continue noncommittal until they are engulfed in the ensuing crescendo. The two stare outside through the window.* ARCHER *closes one eye and mimes shooting at the motorcade with his*

12

fingers. She lowers his hand and mocks a gestural reprimand. The sirens fade and vanish.

ARCHER

The royal motorcade! Always in a rush! Where's the predator going?

MIMUDEH

He must be going to the stadium. This year's Reed Dance, remember? It started eight days ago. This is its eighth and final day.

ARCHER

This explains the influx of tourists in the city. I think I heard Greek, Spanish, Russian and Sicilian spoken by the throngs on Main Street today.

MIMUDEH

Foreigners marvel at our culture. We are a unique nation —a cultural Mecca.

ARCHER

Is the King going to pick a thirteenth, or is it fourteenth wife?

MIMUDEH

He will pick wife Number Thirteen, according to tradition, Archer. In Africa *triskaidekaphobia* has no meaning. What's your take on polygamy, my boy? Does it rock?

ARCHER

(*Nodding, smiling subtly and pointing at her*) That is mischievous of you to ask. Is it a Litmus test, Mimudeh? There isn't polygamy in our family. I am a purebred Briton. Don't tell me you are colour-blind.

MIMUDEH

Polygamy and barbarism flow in everyone's veins, love. What does history say about the Vandals, the Vikings, the Lombardi and the Celtics? At a place called Salmonsby in Gloucestershire, Celtic tribesmen were still eating their womenfolk at the time of Jesus' birth.

ARCHER

That was then, girlfriend...centuries ago when men were beasts and Julius Caesar was God! We are talking *now* –the twenty-first century! It's outdated.

MIMUDEH

If it were, we wouldn't have droves of Swedes, Canadians, Arabs and Britons coming to watch the dance.

ARCHER

In most countries people still flock to watch a beheading or a brutal kick-boxing tournament. We still have people who believe suicide bombers are God-sent. There're bars in Europe were patrons can watch live sex.

MIMUDEH *gasps in shock. But the sirens sound again, booming from the direction they died. The two look through the window again until the noise fades and dies.*

MIMUDEH

Back already? Or the crux of the ceremony was cancelled?

ARCHER

(*Stepping back to snap her again*) I think mamma's boy forgot his dear mother and is going back to fetch her. People say Jirimita can sniff real maidens from fake ones. They say the son is a window-dressing mannequin. She's the empress. Very soon you shall hear the sirens again.

MIMUDEH

(*Laughing*) O! This world of mirages and façades! What if I am also a mannequin?

He waves at her dismissively as she poses clownishly again, and begins to snap her endlessly.

Curtain

Scene Three

Evening of same day
A palatial reception hall

[Act 1]

KING LIMA, *in a tuxedo, and a timid* QUEEN AYOLA *are partying with about a dozen drunken friends; a uniformed Air Marshall and scantily dressed young women. The* ROYAL POET, *in his performance hides carrying a knobkerrie, is drinking from a champagne bottle while performing staccato-style to a disinterested party,* RADIMIR IVANOV, *the Russian butler, is going round with a tray of champagne-filled glasses and packs of cigars. The mood is debauched.*

ROYAL POET
In Ngoloi, a new bride wades away sunset.
A repository greater than any reserve bank,
In her shall the assurance of the dynasty repose.
The Loi watch a mercurial sun rising again at sunset.

Enter CHUCHU, *the royal diviner, followed by* QUEEN MOTHER JIRIMITA. *All the music and dance stop. The diviner is in traditional garbs and carrying a rustic divination bag. The King's mother, draped in a colourful blanket, is in a dark, floor-sweeping dress and beadwork headdress. She is carrying a rolled goatskin under an armpit. The King disentangles himself from* QUEEN AYOLA, *then rises from her sofa and waves everyone away. Exeunt* ALL *except the diviner and the King's mother.*

CHUCHU *spreads the goatskin on the floor and sits on it, her legs spread out. The* QUEEN MOTHER *sits cross-legged besides the diviner who motions the King to sit, which he does a step away on a low ornamental stool, and removes his shoes in reverence. The diviner takes out a corked two-litre concoction bottle from the bag.*

CHUCHU
Roots of sacred trees and the dung of male hippopotami. Start your new marriage with vigour. The celebration can wait. Do you find offence in my coming?

QUEEN MOTHER JIRIMITA
It would be absurd of him to. By tradition and custom, a *sangoma* has precedence. The Lion is a man governed by perceptions. But you see with spiritual eyes –the eyes of the living-dead.

CHUCHU *shakes the bottle, uncorks it, takes a sip, corks it again and hands it to* KING LIMA. *He surveys the bottle and looks at his mother who nods at him. He uncorks the bottle and brings it to his mouth.*

CHUCHU
Always shake it first to agitate the spirits in it.

He re-corks, shakes the bottle, sips and recoils from a bitter taste.

QUEEN MOTHER JIRIMITA
Gulp it, King Lima. It cannot be fouler than the gall bladder of a ram you take at the beginning of every year. It cannot be bitterer than the concoctions you took at your coronation.

KING LIMA *gulps a mouthful of the concoction, his face indifferent. He sets the bottle down.*

CHUCHU
Drink it every night. It is the key to tranquillity in this kingdom and a barricade against uprisings. (*From the bag, she takes out bound roots, shakes her head, puts them back, fumbles and draws a different set*) Put this in your bath every morning. To foreigners you shall be jasmine. To your subjects you shall be red ochre. It'll bring you more charm and fortune. (*Gives him the roots and draws a small, corked and beaded gourd from her bag*) The fat and genitals of a feared lion. A dead witch protects this gourd. Apply the contents to your face. Your enemies shall cringe and flee you on sight. (*Gives him the gourd and fishes a sachet with a ground substance*) Herbs from the Indian Ocean mixed with the skin of a rock python. Spice your food with them. The rock python woos and advances at the same time. (*Appraises him*) You are as astute as your father. On account of my charms and amulets, his backbone turned into steel; that is how he managed to marry over a hundred women concurrently. Ask your mother; I was as dear to him as the air he breathed. (*Begins to pack her things*)

QUEEN MOTHER JIRIMITA
She interrupted your party to test your devotion. A ruler's wisdom and longevity are determined by the importance he vests in his **sangoma**, which are manifestly adherence to traditional advice.

CHUCHU
(*Rises with her bag*) I must give way to foreign reporters. It's the last day of the full moon —the conclusion of this year's

Reed Dance. Foreigners are keen to interview you. Soon you'll hear the bell. Answer their questions elaborately for you'll be speaking to your detractors at home and in far flung parts of the world.

The diviner walks towards the exit and a bell rings. Exeunt CHUCHU. *The bell rings again. As the King hastily puts on his shoes and, almost dashing, stows away everything he received from the diviner, his mother rises from the goatskin, rolls and stows it behind a sofa. She sits in the sofa and adjusts tightly the blanket wrapped around her shoulders.*

KING LIMA
(*Standing. To the door*) Enter!

Enter RADIMIR IVANOV. *He bows at the* QUEEN MOTHER *and then at the King.*

RADIMIR IVANOV
Your Majesty, journalists are in the house for the press conference, as scheduled.

KING LIMA
Show them in, Ivanov. They have ten minutes. (*Crosses to an armchair and sits*) I can't keep my guests and bride waiting, and my mother wants to retire.

The butler bows again. Exeunt IVANOV. *He re-enters ushering* PROF PITONI *followed by a scrum of foreign journalists bearing TV cameras and other recording devices. Under the supervision of the advisor, the reporters quickly mount microphones and sit around him,*

20

some on the carpet. PROF PITONI *finally stands at the seated King's left side.*

Before you ask me any question, I wish to donate to charity as I celebrate the ascension today of a lovely bride, Queen Ayola, into the royal family. (*Draws three bank cheques from an inner pocket in his jacket*) I am donating – (*Reads*)
US\$20 000 to the Ngoloi Association of People with Disabilities, US\$10 000 to the Albino Association of Ngoloi and **US\$5 000 to Ngongoza Old People's Home**. I am not a very wealthy man; otherwise I would have donated more generously. (*Passes the cheques to* PROF PITONI)

WHITE JOURNALIST (MALE)
I am Rowland Collins – CNN. Your Majesty, some Loi in the Diaspora and many Americans think that the Reed Dance is sheer extravagance and reeks of immorality. What would be your take on that, Sir?

KING LIMA
Extravagance is the amassing of nuclear and ballistic missiles that will destroy mankind. Extravagance is when billions of dollars, euro and roubles are spent trying to investigate if ever there was life on Mars when research for diseases like cancer and AIDS needs more funding. Immorality is the parades of half-naked neo-Sodomites that happen annually in London, Johannesburg and New York City. Immorality is the men and women who undergo transsexual operations, and the diabolic surgeons who alter them.

CHINESE JOURNALIST (FEMALE)

My name is Chen Heng working for Xinhua of China. Deducing from your statement, it appears you begrudge the spending patterns of superpowers, or the freedoms practised in them. Sir, is it a question of sour grapes or you are against Moscow, Washington and Beijing?

QUEEN MOTHER JIRIMITA

(*Crossing from the sofa and coming to stand at the seated King's right side*) He is against journalists who think they can use the pen to blot a people's culture. (*As focus shifts to her, flashlights blind her momentarily*) He is against foreigners who judge our culture by their flawed standards when back home their way of life is wicked and their priests preside over gay marriages. The Lion is against organisations that spend millions of dollars protecting gorillas and chimpanzees when thousands of people are starving in Africa and Asia.

WHITE JOURNALIST (MALE)

Rowland once again, Madam. From what you've just said, Queen Mother, wouldn't one be tempted to believe you've an ingenious propensity to change the subject?

QUEEN MOTHER JIRIMITA

I don't see how our definition of profligacy and debauchery and his perspective at the world would tempt any level-headed American. Our culture has nothing to do with the financial meltdown in the euro zone. The Lion is not responsible for the bloody squabbles in the Middle East. Some of you are considering blaming global warming and the depletion of the Ozone layer on the Reed Dance.

A brief, nervous giggle erupts in the scrum.

ARABIC JOURNALIST (MALE)
My name is Jibril Hakimi standing for Al Jazeera. Sir, this kingdom is infamous for its poor human rights record while your opulence is in sharp contrast to the abject poverty in the rural areas. Are you aware of the possible criminal injustices you and your courts of law could be committing, or is it a lie that sixty-nine per cent of the Loi live below the poverty-datum line?

KING LIMA
(*Giggles*) What did Christ say about poverty and the poor? He said the poor shall always be in your midst. Although the Church of England is my religion, I am averse to the Anglicization of our culture.

WHITE JOURNALIST (FEMALE)
My name is Catherine Boyd –BBC. Sir, what does the head of the Church of England say about polygamy? Doesn't he think you stand condemned in the eyes of God?

QUEEN MOTHER JIRIMITA
Rather, my daughter, you should seek to establish what Christ said pertaining to culture, not what the head of the Church of England thinks. The archbishop of Canterbury is a man and fallible by definition. Your answer lies in the circumcision of Jesus and His Jewish upbringing. A person's culture is their natural religion; it dictates norms for them.

WHITE JOURNALIST (FEMALE**)**

I am Irina Zhavoronkov–*Russia Today*. The UN Secretary General once told a press conference that he was considering scheduling a meeting with you to discuss human rights abuses, especially the incarceration of local journalists in your prisons. Are you going to meet him, Sir?

QUEEN MOTHER JIRIMITA

I suppose it would be noble of His Majesty to meet the UN leader after the world body has silenced the gunfire in the ceaselessly troubled spots of the world. At any rate, we have a functional judiciary system in this kingdom. Whoever is in our prisons was fairly tried and convicted within the framework of our sovereign laws. Should the Secretary's hands prove full, he could send a special envoy to investigate. I am confident the Lion of Ngoloi will be more than pleased to take the envoy on a tour of our prisons. (*Glances at her wristwatch*) I am afraid that was all the time he had for you.

PROF PITONI *waves the journalists away.* KING LIMA *rises, adjusts his necktie and tuxedo and, smiling, bows civilly amid the flashing lights of cameras. Shortly, he and his mother walk towards the exit. Exeunt* KING LIMA *and the* QUEEN MOTHER.

Curtain

Act Two

Scene One

Midday
An executive boardroom

KATOMENE, *an Opposition* PRESIDENT, TAJI, *ten members, including a few whites, and a* MUSCULAR BODYGUARD *are sitting around a boardroom table. The bodyguard, in a black suit and tight T-shirt, is standing slightly behind the chairperson. A political party logo is on a wall behind the chairman. On the opposite wall is a red banner written: NGOLOI DEMOCRATIC PARTY (NDP).*

KATOMENE
President, we need foreign intervention. I suggest we bring our case before the UN Security Council.

PRESIDENT
Hon. Hasa, there isn't open war in this kingdom, which makes our case of no significance to the Security Council. Even in deserving situations like the genocide of Rwanda, the feuding that ravaged Somalia and the bloodshed that swept Syria, the UN took long to act. We must not put too much faith in foreign intervention.

KATOMENE
But it is not by submitting that the NDP will force the King to renounce the monarchy. It's time the people of this country roared at the Lion of Ngoloi.

PRESIDENT

I'll not allow a direct confrontation. Those versed in defensive driving will tell you that a head-on collision must be avoided at any cost.

KATOMENE

I won't be far from the truth if I say the masses want to demonstrate and die for this country. You could put it to the vote, sir.

PRESIDENT

We don't want a Red Sunday or Monday on our soil, Hon. Hasa. Everyone in this boardroom knows we have an amuck Riot Police in this country. The Royal Guard is a cluster of trigger-happy lunatics.

TAJI

(*Rises, perplexed*) But you must make the meeting decide.

PRESIDENT

We are fighting repression and violence, Mr Taji; therefore I won't approve violence. The puppet government approved our party on the basis of our non-aggressive cordiality as stated in our constitution.

TAJI

Uprisings are synonymous with death. People usually die to bring about change.

PRESIDENT

Sit down, Mr Taji. Let others speak. That horse is dead.

TAJI

Not until you put it to the vote, sir. And I am sure we need to revisit our constitution. It cannot continue to read like that of the Curia. We are not cardinals and I don't want to think you are vying for the papal office.

PRESIDENT

I've already said 'no'. My 'no' is a considered, temperate response.

TAJI

Heroic camaraderie and sacrifice do not seem to apply here.

PRESIDENT

We have no armed wing; therefore the only route for us is the Dalai Lama approach –love and aggressive persuasion. I see no merit in your line of argument. If we urged people to take to the streets, the executive shall be hunted down like animals of the chase, and killed. Those among us with some streak of luck will be detained, tortured to half-wits and released after several months.

TAJI

Sir, Ngoloi and the Loi are burning. How do we make love in a burning house? This isn't time for romance.

PRESIDENT

Emotions are responsible for every war ever fought. (*Emphatic*) Factual, meritorious practicality, not emotions, will bring us democracy.

TAJI

You are wrong, Mr President. Emotions gave birth to the Long March, the Red October Revolution ...the sovereignty of every nation. Without emotions ambitions can't exist.

PRESIDENT

Sit down, Mr Taji, or I'll hold you in contempt. I do not have the time today for a philosophical showdown.

TAJI

I'll not be counted among timid millipedes. (*Schizophrenic*) We formed NDP because life was no longer worth living. The Ruling Party and the Government are for window-dressing. We are persecuted, hunted and killed every day. From the twenty-seventh of August until yesterday, the world shamelessly watched the cleavages of our daughters gyrating for the King. (*Bangs a fist on the table*) I'll fight the autocrat alone. I resign!

PRESIDENT

While we pray that God above destroys the satanic dynasty, and rebuilds what the fool destroyed, you are free to resign. Freedom of choice is the essence of what we are fighting for. But I must warn you, Mr Taji; the King is a very lethal man far from the charmer that you see on television.

TAJI

Death is of no consequence to an oppressed man. (*More schizophrenic*) Peasants rose against Nicholas II, and butchered him! Kabila chased Mobutu Sese Seko, the Lion of Zaire, out of his palace like a jaguarondi! Then the looting started. The Congolese took back what the tyrant had stolen from them.

Taji quickly picks his dairy, a folder and some papers. He snatches his suit jacket draped on the backrest of his chair, and storms towards the exit. Exeunt TAJI.

PRESIDENT

(*Sighs*) Sorry about that, ladies and gentlemen. Ever since he was involved in that road accident he has become a hurricane.

KATOMENE

Of course, he is disturbed, but we need a little aggression. Our efforts in parliament are a verbal, fruitless token.

PRESIDENT

We can't afford to lose lives knowingly. (*Glances at his wristwatch*) Meeting adjourned to 14:00 hrs. Thank you.

Some members rise, some pack their papers and folders, while the BODYGUARD *draws back the leader's chair and the* PRESIDENT *rises.*

Curtain

Scene Two

Morning
A palatial patio

[Act 2]

In the room immaculate with red roses and other flowers in gigantic vases, KING LIMA *attended by* QUEEN LILIOSA *and* QUEEN AMINA, *is watching a white* STRIPTEASE DANCER *performing on a pole. The King is topless and wrapped in a towel from the waist downwards. The two queens are in towels too. Heavy metal rock is playing on a portable CD player beside the monarch. The dancer is shedding clothes and swinging on the pole. The King, nursing and sipping a cocktail, is reclining in a deck chair, his symbolic spear leaning on a table nearby.* QUEEN LILIOSA *is giving him a pedicure while* QUEEN AMINA *is oiling and combing his hair, and massaging his scalp.*

A bell rings. The King turns his head in dismay while the dancer continues unabated. Enter RADIMIR IVANOV *followed by* PROF PITONI, *the latter carrying an executive briefcase. Both stop a pace into the room and bow. The butler motions the professor to proceed to the King. Exeunt* IVANOV. PROF PITONI *crosses to the King.*

PROF PITONI
Good morning, Your Majesty. (*To the queens*) Your Highnesses, I recognise you.

The queens nod and continue their attendance.

31

KING LIMA

What brings you here, Prof Pitoni?

PROF PITONI

(*Standing forlornly*) There is something you must know, Sir. Most urgent I must say, or you would deem me grossly incompetent.

KING LIMA

Tell me, learned one. By reading tomes at Oxford and fathoming the depths of knowledge, my left ear is ever yours. But my right one is devoted to the oracles. (*Laughs*) Between them is a Sherburne-sharpened brain for balance.

PROF PITONI

(*Shrugs bafflement*) Of course, Your Majesty. That is what makes the Lion of Ngoloi a natural wonder that awes the continent. But, Sovereign, I am afraid the material is for your ears only.

KING LIMA

But this is Queen Liliosa and Queen Amina.

PROF PITONI

The matter demands privacy or it will be in the newspapers too soon. Lately you've been in the *Tribune* and *Sunday Times* for the wrong reasons.

KING LIMA *sits up and motions to the queens to wind up.* QUEEN LILIOSA *dries his feet, slips them into a pair of sandals and massages his calves.* QUEEN AMINA *covers him with a batik cloth. The King nods dismissively at the queens who rise and saunter towards the exit. Exeunt* QUEEN LILIOSA *and* AMINA. *The King lowers the volume of the CD player, and looks questioningly at his advisor. The dancer continues to striptease and swing.*

PROF PITONI
(*Motions at the dancer*) We need total privacy, Sir.

KING LIMA
You also dare interrupt my entertainment! I guess you aren't here to force me to reason like a pure American democrat. (*Points at an ornate low stool*) Political rhetoric is rather untoward on a merry Friday. Sit down, Professor, and perform your office.

The royal advisor sits on the stool and sets his briefcase down. Enter IVANOV *with a cocktail on a tray. He presents the cocktail to* PROF PITONI *and bows. Exeunt* IVANOV. *The professor sips the beverage and sets it on a table. The King turns the CD player off and motions the dancer, now down to a scant bikini suit, to leave. Hastily, she picks her strewn clothes. Exeunt the* STRIPTEASE DANCER.

This is the sixth of September. The dust of the Reed dance has not yet settled. Some of the maidens wore the feathers of the bishop bird –the bird's fluffs are still adrift. (*Edgy*) King Lima is listening, Prof Pitoni.

PROF PITONI
Katomene Hasa shocked the House of Assembly yesterday. He moved a motion that intends to abolish the Reed Dance.

33

KING LIMA

When I wanted to ban the Opposition, you, my learned political advisor, said I sounded worse than a blend of Adolf Hitler, Pol Pot and Jorge Videla. Now this Katomene, African as I am, denounces our culture! (*Pauses*) Where was the Minister of Culture and Tourism when this comedian was speaking?

PROF PITONI

He protested strongly, but in vain. The Speaker of Parliament threatened to throw the MP out.

KING LIMA

The Speaker sympathises with the Opposition. Suppose you ran a poultry farm and happened to discover a Gabon viper among your chicken, what would you do, Professor?

PROF PITONI

Sir, there was no room for the Speaker to bend the rules.

Enter QUEEN MOTHER JIRIMITA *ethereally dressed, but in gloomy colours.*

QUEEN MOTHER JIRIMITA

(*Walking about*) I overheard your conversation, honourable gentlemen. The Speaker should've used his doctorate to act in the best interest of the kingdom. You are also a learned man, Your Majesty; you are an old Shirburnian. Real education lies in understanding one's culture and appreciating it. Academic knowledge does not make an African wiser. We have lost wisdom through civilisation. Katomene Hasa will force the Lion to dissolve Parliament.

PROF PITONI

That would be disastrous, my good sister. He cannot follow in your husband's footsteps. Parliament is an essential pillar of democracy –

QUEEN MOTHER JIRIMITA

Democracy! Is that word glued to your tongue? (*Grabs the King's spear. Angrily*) He is King Lima III; a descendent of fighters and conquerors! His forefathers fell in battle for this throne! (*Fiery, pacing*) Where was democracy in 1750, my brother? Was it an embryo in the womb of an undocumented Mary? Where was it?

PROF PITONI

Please calm down, Queen Mother. I beg you to sit down, Your Highness.

QUEEN MOTHER JIRIMITA

Don't calm me down, Pitoni! I am not a Californian veldt fire! This Katomene (*grins*) do unto him the opposite of what the Psalmist prophesied about the Saviour: *He keepeth all his bones: not one of them is broken.* I hear the litany of a verse in my mind: *Yea, his soul draweth near unto the grave, and his life to the destroyers.* I want all his bones broken. (*Looks at the King*) Decree it so, Great Lion.

Tense silence prevails momentarily. The King sighs in exasperation and rises aimlessly.

PROF PITONI

Great Lion of Ngoloi, Bearer of sacred symbols, thou shall not kill. Murder is unjust.

QUEEN MOTHER JIRIMITA

Don't confuse him, Professor. He is running a kingdom, not the Church of England. You would honour his sensibilities by leaving such sermons to the archbishop of Canterbury.

PROF PITONI

Queen Mother, if something happened to the legislator everyone would suspect the monarch.

KING LIMA

My subjects wouldn't suspect me. I tithe religiously. Of course, I own palaces and lodges, but they aren't Khmer Rouge hide-outs. I donate to charity and marry poor commoners. Katomene is a politician; he has many friends and many foes. People will suspect a Brutus in his own party.

QUEEN MOTHER JIRIMITA

The MP, by sharpening a machete against His Majesty, has turned himself into an enemy of God and the ancestors. And you, my brother, by defending a treasonous character, you make my son see you as his sworn Judas.

KING LIMA

(*Plucks a rosebud. Looking at it*) Christ was a man of profound leniency; He knowingly kept the company of a man He knew would betray Him. Unlike Him, I squash my enemies, both real and imagined. (*Squashes the bud, lets its sepals and petals slip through his fingers and tramples them*) This day, Friday the sixth of September, I decree the legislator's death. I want him in a body bag by Monday.

PROF PITONI
My advice is in good faith and professional; I am your
uncle.

QUEEN MOTHER JIRIMITA
Thank the white man for his education, Professor. In
ancestral times a maternal uncle of your calibre was a
nincompoop. You are yet to kill a lion or a human being.
Why can't you be like him; he holds education and tradition
in different hands. By his own hand he circumcised himself.

PROF PITONI *suffers an asthmatic attack. Panting, he hastily
loosens his necktie and fetches an inhaler from the briefcase.* KING
LIMA *and the* QUEEN MOTHER *watch indifferently as he
breathes laboriously.*

KING LIMA
This kingdom needs real men who can defend it from
globalisation. It does not need uncles yet to prove their
bravery. Very soon Stars and Stripes shall fly on every piece
of land under the sun if men like you won't remove colonial
blinkers. Instead of a multiplicity of knowledge steeling you
in our culture, it has ossified you.

Still inhaling, PROF PITONI *slightly stabilises.*

QUEEN MOTHER JIRIMITA
Clearly an Oxford PhD has raised you above animal
existence, but it did nothing to teach you subordination to
authority. It taught you to analyse the past and contemplate
the future, but it was silent on African peculiarities. I am
tempted to believe your lecturers deliberately omitted to tell

you that the English have evolved the principles of freedom for over seven hundred and fifty years now. We are African and newcomers in that area. (*With severity*) You heard the decree, my learned brother. His Majesty only honours the warlike. You've an entire weekend to perform the decree. Now take your leave and stop his heart from bleeding further.

The professor remains seated. The QUEEN MOTHER *poses and sets to throw the spear at him, at which point the professor rises, picks his briefcase and crosses to the exit. Exeunt* PROF PITONI. *The* QUEEN MOTHER *crosses to the King, curtsies and hands him the spear.*

Curtain

Scene Three

Afternoon
The legislator's lounge-cum-dining room

[Act 2]

The MP's wife, BELEMINA, *is in an apron dusting glassware. Enter a dejected* KATOMENE *carrying some folders, a briefcase and a suit jacket.*

BELEMINA
Hello. (*Wipes hands on apron*) How was your day? (*Crosses to meet him, grabs his necktie, pulls him to her and kisses him on the lips*) You don't look fine? (*Relieves him of the items*)

KATOMENE
It's terrible. Didn't you watch the news?

BELEMINA
I was busy. We must hire a maid before my vacation ends.

He stirs her gently to the lounge section and sits in a sofa while she sets the folders and briefcase on a table and the jacket on the backrest of a chair. She crosses to sit on his sofa's armrest.

BELEMINA
What happened?

KATOMENE
They killed Mr Taji… in cold blood.

BELEMINA

Jesus! How? Couldn't they see that his brain was a corkscrew?

KATOMENE

He tried to take placards into the city. (*Sighs*) A government pathologist counted twenty-one bullet wounds in his upper body alone.

BELEMINA

Lima ought to be ashamed. (*Begins to undo his necktie*) They shot him in public?

KATOMENE

No. His placard-festooned car broke down in a secluded spot outside the city. Taji lived on a farm, remember. I am sure they shot him on the spot. Then the police took his body for display along Main Street, along with a grenade and a loaded pistol as exhibits. The man never owned any weapon. The grenade and the pistol are Government Issue. Police Ass. Insp. Loebbe Koro described Taji as a man who craved martyrdom. He said the Royal Guard shot him when he tried to bulldoze his way into the King's main palace. They displayed his body as a deterrent.

BELEMINA

God forbid! His wife shouldn't have left him after the car accident. She could've stopped him.

KATOMENE

His mental state had become unbearable. There is something you must know, Belemina. Yesterday I denounced the Reed Dance in Parliament. I actually moved the motion.

BELEMINA

Christ in Heaven! What had crept into you?

KATOMENE

I cannot watch from the margins while a man abuses innocent girls.

BELEMINA

An MP is not a messiah, Katomene. An MP isn't an Imam.

KATOMENE

I had Mimudeh and Yemudeh in mind when I moved the motion. How can a person of my stature close his eyes while Ngoloi burns?

BELEMINA

People shut up for the sake of their families. Lima has the army, the police, the Secret Service and an anarchic militia at his disposal. The American ambassador can sneak us out of the country before Monday.

KATOMENE

That would be overreacting. We'll see Chuchu. The *sangoma* will assist us.

BELEMINA

We are back to sorcerers again! When are we going to be proper Catholics?

KATOMENE

You are an accountant, Belemina; you know the importance of flexibility.

BELEMINA

But she is the Royal *Sangoma*. She is bound to tell the King everything.

KATOMENE

I've already called her on the phone. She'll be here tomorrow night. I'll pay her handsomely.

Enter MIMUDEH *carrying a History textbook. She is in ordinary clothes.*

MIMUDEH

Hi, Dad.

KATOMENE

Hi, Mimudeh. Hope you had a great day at school. But I discern a question on your face.

MIMUDEH

Yeah. Dad, did we pass through the Jurassic Age or we are descendants of Adam and Eve? (*Browsing the book*) It seems a fact that we evolved. This book is full of pictures of archaeological facts.

KATOMENE

(*Smiles*) For distinctions in your subjects you mustn't mix archaeology with religion. The two are perpetually antagonistic —fire and water, light and darkness, ancient tradition and civilisation. You can't square a circle, my daughter.

Confounded, Mimudeh crosses to them to show him the evidence.

Curtain

Act Three

Scene One

Night
Inside Chuchu's rustic shrine

KING LIMA, *barefoot in distinct African attire, is seated on a low wooden stool facing* CHUCHU. *The diviner is in a black cloth, beads, anklets, etc, and a printed red headscarf. Gourds, effigies, troughs, hides, spiritual cloths, etc, are on the floor and the wall. In a trance, she casts divination bones on a goatskin and studies them.*

CHUCHU

(*Looking at the bones*) I see a hyena eating a hyena...a bat eating a bat. I see blood on the throne. (*Looks at him*) I see two spears in a blacksmith's furnaces.

KING LIMA

Shed more light, *Sangoma*. Make plain what you see. Whose blood is on the throne? What are the two spears and what are they doing in the fire?

CHUCHU

(*Gathers the bones and casts them again*) The blood I see on the throne is yours. I see it on the floor and on the palace walls like gloom petals. You've enemies in the palace, outside the palace and overseas. I see war, hunger and strife. I see you and your wives running amok naked in the streets. (*She swills water in her mouth from a gourd, takes an animal skull, studies it and spits the water in a jet onto the skull*) Beware of Ngoloi Catholics

45

and their bishop. (*Pauses*) Take time to learn from the cockerel. I see decadence in the palace and outside the palace.

KING LIMA
Sangoma, enlighten me on the two spears and the furnaces.

CHUCHU
One furnace is being fanned by a man in a wig; the other is between the feet of a man whose clothes are chameleonic. But your hands are poking the embers.

In an attitude of supplication, the King draws a wad of money from a pocket and places it before the diviner.

(*Growls and smiles*) The spirits and the gods are your bulwarks. When the time comes, follow your instinct for that is how you shall overcome. Instinct is instruction from the unborn and the dead.

CHUCHU *chants incorrigibly for a moment and points dismissively at the exit.*

Curtain

Scene Two

Same night
A palatial drawing-room

[Act 3]

The QUEEN MOTHER, *tacit and wrapped in a dark blanket, is in a rocking chair by a lit hearth.* RADIMIR IVANOV *ushers* PROF PITONI *into the lounge. Both bow in unison towards the queen who appears oblivious of their presence. Exeunt* IVANOV. *The advisor stands forlornly looking down at her across the room.*

QUEEN MOTHER JIRIMITA

(*To the fire*)Upon my instincts I prevailed on His Majesty to oblige the Commander-General to swear his allegiance again, despite his earlier oath in January. The third was the last day of the full moon, the last day of the Reed Dance –the most awe-inspiring cultural event on the continent. Over forty thousand maidens attended. Two days after the ascension of a rural commoner, a legislator makes an absurd proposal. (*Pauses and looks up at him*) The brass tacks are quite simple. The motion to ban a dance that instils good morals in our girls cannot be the MP's idea. This is the reason I came to stay here for a while. A hunch tells me things aren't right. We are going to leave our memorial, not in stupid marble statues like the Romans did, but in an imperishable culture and a versatile tradition. (*Motions to a chair in front of her*)

PROF PITONI *sits facing her. Re-enter* IVANOV *with tea. The butler quickly fills two cups and bows. Exeunt* IVANOV.

No Reed Dance, no tourists, no foreign currency. It translates to overtaxing the worker which breeds civil unrest. I breathe politics; I once served as regent following my husband's death. The Crown Prince was still a boy then. You'll recall that I sent him to Sherburne to study.

PROF PITONI

I am the one who accompanied him to England. He was the protégé from the beginning. You took the reins until he was eighteen years old. Now he is the head of State and Government. As an enlightened Anglican, he knows the sacredness of human life. We must not forge a devil out of him. God wouldn't exonerate us.

QUEEN MOTHER JIRIMITA

If you perused the Holy Bible, the Al Koran or the Bhagavad-Gita, for instance, you would learn that God created when it was time to create, and destroyed when it was time to destroy. The Exodus isn't over yet, my brother. Pharaoh now has sundry names –NATO, democracy, civilisation, good governance, and etcetera. Sift through the flowery terms and you'll unmask political hegemony. Do I speak your language, my brother?

PROF PITONI

You do, Queen Mother, but we can't have a legislator killed for speaking in Parliament. A familiar humaneness should dictate the safeguard of human life to us all. And it wasn't the Reed Dance that he was against. He denounced the King's acquisition of maidens.

QUEEN MOTHER JIRIMITA

Every royal family has its culture and peculiarities. We are as cultural as the royal households of Britain, the Netherlands or Japan. Other nations must respect us. For God's sake, we aren't Aghori cannibals.

PROF PITONI

Your Highness, absolute rule has no place in the modern world. (*Sips the tea and sets the cup down*) Our critics say there is no rule of law in Ngoloi because the King's brain is between his legs.

QUEEN MOTHER JIRIMITA

You are irretrievably out of bounds, my brother! Let His Majesty enjoy his father's sweat. His father petitioned the British Crown and toppled the concessionaires. His father persuaded the British to grant us our Independence.

PROF PITONI

It is difficult enough for a man to satisfy one wife — thirteen, unworkable!

QUEEN MOTHER JIRIMITA

(*Sips her tea and nurses the cup*) Every nation has its gods. The stone circles at Avebury and Stonehenge in Britain are pagan altars. Polygamy and several children is the ambrosia for our gods.

PROF PITONI

The concurrent marriages your husband entered into were our foxy colonisers' scheme of merriment for your husband —to plague his mind with domestic squabbles.

Behind him they fuelled the concessions that made our people and the Government landless.

QUEEN MOTHER JIRIMITA
I see you are headstrong. You stubbornly deny facts and you try not to be anybody's lackey. But you heard the decree yesterday. This is Saturday; soon it shall be Monday.

PROF PITONI
Spare him, Your Highness. Hatchet jobs are Bronze Age. You are a Christian. I came to appeal to you.

QUEEN MOTHER JIRIMITA
Prof Pitoni, can a woman festooned with charms and amulets be a born-again? (*Shows him talismanic anklets and wrist bands on her person*) A favoured man in your position brings bacon home by executing His Majesty's decrees –that is the beaten track.

PROF PITONI
But you were baptised and christened Miriam.

QUEEN MOTHER JIRIMITA
Christ was baptised too, but they killed Him. Make it appear as if he died in a car crash. Or submit his body to the Hoffmanns.

PROF PITONI
You've had many people killed, Queen Mother. Aren't you tired?

QUEEN MOTHER JIRIMITA

That is neither here nor there, Pitoni. (*Rises*)You stand in the league of our detractors and speak their language. The day the Lima dynasty goes down is the day all of us will go down. (*Magisterial*) The next Reed Dance goes ahead as scheduled no matter what Parliament decides.

PROF PITONI

Queen Mother, Parliament makes the law.

QUEEN MOTHER JIRIMITA

My son is the Law! He is its spirit and its life! By Monday you'll break to us the news of Katomene's death. You are dismissed, learned one.

The professor rises and bows. The QUEEN MOTHER, *still standing, watches him crossing to the exit. Exeunt* PROF PITONI.

Curtain

Scene Three

Same night
The legislator's lounge-cum-dining room

[Act 3]

In their pyjamas, KATOMENE *and* BELEMINA, *both yawning, the former reading a newspaper, the latter working on her nails, are huddled in a sofa. A blanket covers their feet. Both keep glancing at their wristwatches.*

BELEMINA
People say Chuchu rose from the dead. I am scared of her, dear. What time is she coming?

KATOMENE
She didn't say. Any minute I guess. The *Sangoma* might deliver us from bondage.

Enter MIMUDEH *going through a bagpipe drum major's paces and waving her mace in a gym skirt, leggings and a T-shirt. The girl marches the length and breadth of the lounge.* BELEMINA *shakes her head in mute disapproval.*

BELEMINA
(*To* MIMUDEH) Will you stop this Scottish madness? There is no future for you in bagpipe music.

MIMUDEH
(*Stops and shrugs*) Come on, Mum. You always look down upon *everything* I do.

BELEMINA

Because you are sixteen, but your behaviour is kindergarten all the time. Yemudeh is not like you. Your twin is studious. We sent her to a boarding school as a result. (*Glances at her watch*) You ought to be studying. Do you still want to become a lawyer?

MIMUDEH

But you said Yemudeh was dull and needed close attention. You favour her *so-o* much, Mum. (*Stands akimbo*) Nonetheless, what should I lecture you on... demography ...types of insurance and their functions...formulae of algebraic equations? Perhaps you would want to hear me recite Mark Anthony's eulogy at Caesar's burial –

BELEMINA

Whoa, Mimudeh! Give us a break this weekend. Won't you?

Marching and swinging the mace, exeunt MIMUDEH. *The doorbell rings. Both stare in the direction of the door.* KATOMENE *puts the newspaper away, rises and draws a pistol from the back of his trousers.*

KATOMENE

(*Whispering*) If it's a stranger tell them I am not around.

BELEMINA

Get it, Katomene. I am scared.

The bell rings again.

KATOMENE

They want me and won't touch you.

She rises and nervously crosses to the door. He follows her and takes a vantage position on its side. She looks at him for assurance. He nods at her. The bell rings for the third time.

BELEMINA

(*To the door*) Who is it?

CHUCHU'S VOICE (OFF-STAGE**)**

(*Parodying sarcastically*) **Who is it? Who is it?** It is I, Chu-chu!

Relieved, KATOMENE *stows the pistol in his pyjamas.* BELEMINA *unbolts and opens the door. Enter* CHUCHU *carrying a rolled goatskin and her non-descript bag. She is still in a black cloth, beads, anklets, etc, and the printed red headscarf. She stops a few paces inside.*

BELEMINA

Sangoma, I greet you.

CHUCHU

The spirit tells me you had a Caesarean birth thirty-seven years ago. Does it lie?

BELEMINA

(*Awe-struck*)No, it does not.

KATOMENE

I sincerely greet you, *Sangoma*.

CHUCHU

I greet you too, Katomene. You come from a lineage of men known for their courage. Your father killed nineteen leopards in his lifetime. Your mother died while delivering you on a reed mat. Does the spirit see well?

KATOMENE, *dumbfounded, bows, his hands clasped, and motions* CHUCHU *to sit where she would please. The diviner sets shop in the centre of the room; sits down and spreads her divination items on the goatskin. The couple sit in the sofa, holding hands, staring at her. The diviner grunts once and slips into a trance, whistling and waving an animal tail. But she suddenly lashes their ankles with the tail, pointing at their stompers, which they quickly remove and throw away. Using the tail,* CHUCHU *points at positions near her for them to sit. The couple complies.*

CHUCHU

Katomene Hasa, son of Hasa, Hasa son of Gada, Gada son of Gadaga, I see you lying in a grave. You provoked the Lion of Ngoloi.

KATOMENE

I seek a way out of my predicament. Protect me, *Sangoma*.

CHUCHU

(*Casts bones on the goatskin*) Make peace with him before he breaks all your bones.

KATOMENE

How do I make peace with a man who wants to kill me?

CHUCHU

The strength of a crocodile lies in the river. What is the best time to kill a crocodile?

KATOMENE

(*Exchanges glances with* BELEMINA) When it is basking in the sun.

CHUCHU

In public, kiss him like a woman you love. How do you draw a crocodile from a river?

KATOMENE

You use bait —usually a small goat, *Sangoma*.

CHUCHU

Use your daughter, but spice her with lethal poison.

KATOMENE

How do I spice my daughter with poison?

CHUCHU

Your enemy is full of staggering lust, which maddens him like a boar.

KATOMENE

But how do I spice my daughter with poison?

CHUCHU

Inhabitants of the earth's coldest regions reckoned how to live on snow. Baboons mastered the art of eating live scorpions without being beaten. Interrogate your mind on how you'll spice your daughter with venom.

KATOMENE *nods at* BELEMINA *who rises and exits. Reenter* BELEMINA *momentarily with two wads of Ngoloi banknotes, which she hands to her husband and resumes her position.* KATOMENE *places the money before* CHUCHU.

KATOMENE
Great *Sangoma*, I've a proposal.

CHUCHU
I know what you desire. You want me to kill the Great Lion.

KATOMENE
You and this monster are cheek and jowl.

CHUCHU
(*Pushes the money away in a rage*) Give me one of your daughters. After the deed, I'll sacrifice her for the appeasement of the wrath of God. Only then will I state my payment, which can be a cow, a handful of coins, or your other daughter. (*Packing her paraphernalia in a huff*) I regret setting foot in this house. You are thrift with your children as if you own them when they are God's. (*Rises and glares at them*) I shall inform the Lion of your wish to see him dead.

The couple, dumbfounded, kneel in humility, the legislator first.

KATOMENE

Do not crucify me, *Sangoma*. It was just a proposal. Please, forgive me.

CHUCHU

No spirit ever forgives. If it were so, Judas Iscariot wouldn't have burst open in the Field of Blood.

KATOMENE

(*Boldly, rising*) You are a dangerous heretic! We'll not entertain a blasphemous witch-doctor! Get out of my house! (*Draws the pistol and aims it at her*) Get-out-now!!!

CHUCHU *retreats slowly.* BELEMINA *rises.*

BELEMINA

Have you lost your mind, Katomene? Put the gun away. Put it away, please.

KATOMENE

(*Aiming with both hands*) To hell with her! She is part of Lima's killing machinery.

CHUCHU

(*Stops retreating and laughs*)You cannot kill me, coward. You are not as brave as your forefathers. (*Spreads her arms*) Shoot me through the heart and prove me wrong.

BELEMINA

Why won't you just go, *Sangoma*?

CHUCHU

I want my body taken to the morgue from here. (*Hysterical*) Send me to the next world! Send me now! Hey! Hey! I beseech you! I beg you! Send me now!

BELEMINA *bulldozes* KATOMENE *away and returns to face* CHUCHU.

BELEMINA

(*Into her face, furious*) You are now trespassing! Whether you are going to report this to Lima or your hobgoblins just go! Or you invite my anger!

CHUCHU

Let me see it! What is the shape and colour of the anger of a woman who entered into holy matrimony aware her vineyard had long been trampled by several men? Two of them were married and you knew it. Your husband was number eh –

CHUCHU *is about to count the men off her fingers when* BELEMINA *slaps her hard on the cheek. The diviner rubs the cheek and, panting, inspects her hand.*

BELEMINA

Your services are no longer required!

The diviner, without exposing herself, quickly rips off her pair of panties and casts them at BELEMINA's *feet. Teary and ferociously angry,* CHUCHU *retreats towards the exit.*

CHUCHU

(*Pointing at them with one hand and groping for the door with the other*) I curse this family! I curse you a thousand times!

Slamming the door behind her, exeunt CHUCHU *without her belongings. The couple stare at the diviner's bag and panties.* KATOMENE *shakes his head and tucks away the pistol.*

KATOMENE

What did you do, Belemina?

BELEMINA

(*Fuming*) **What did I do?** You should've shot her–period! Why do you tolerate demons?

KATOMENE

You *really* wanted me to kill her?

BELEMINA

Why do you keep a weapon you won't use? We are now between the barbarians and the sea.

They stare at each other, KATOMENE *in disbelief.* BELEMINA *sobs and sits in a sofa. He sinks dejectedly beside her and sighs endlessly.*

(*Mournfully*) O! By inviting her you erred. But by sparing her life you reasoned. I am sorry I became emotional. O! We could've been in a situation now. (*Wiping tears with her hands*) Are we going to cut and run? What about our livelihoods? What about our children?

Enter MIMUDEH *in a huff and unplugging earphones from her ears.*

MIMUDEH
What's the matter, Dad? Who came? I think I heard quarrelling. (*Pointing at the bag and panties*) What's going on, Mum?

BELEMINA
You won't understand it, Mimudeh. Please go back to your room.

The girl is baffled. Exeunt MIMUDEH. *After a moment of demurring,* BELEMINA *exits and re-enters shortly with a porridge stick, which she uses to pick the panties and carefully places them in the diviner's bag. She crosses to a window, opens it and throws away the stick.*

Curtain

Act Four

Scene One

Sunday morning
A palatial lounge

QUEEN LILIOSA *enters wrapped in a towel, a smaller one covering her hair. She is carrying a tube of lotion and an exquisite bottle of perfume. On an ornamental table is a pile of different newspapers. She sets the perfume and the lotion on a low stool near a sofa, places a foot on the stool and sensually fingers the length of her leg upwards. Then she begins to apply lotion to her leg.*

QUEEN LILIOSA

(*Sensually, applying the lotion*) Wasted beauty.... Had it not been for the wealth, I wouldn't have married him. Rarely does he remember that I am his wife. When he does and comes to my quarters, he is too tired. (*Straightens and caresses her breasts*) O! How I want to be touched… How I want the fire inside me extinguished…Thirteen wives… his hands are full (*Looks at her fundament and applies lotion to the other leg*) Crème de la crème… A lady of my calibre should not be starved. How I yearn to hold my own child–royal blood. (*Finishes applying make-up seated in a sofa, a mirror in her hand and a make-up kit on her lap*) Butler! Butler! Mr Ivanov!

Enter IVANOV and stands still before her, but respectfully looking away.

63

IVANOV

(*Bowing*) At your service, Your Highness.

QUEEN LILIOSA

(*Making-up, without looking at him*) Bring me my favourite burgundy.

Exeunt IVANOV.

Mr Ivanov! Radimir Ivanov!

Re-enter IVANOV *again and stands still.*

IVANOV

(*Bowing*) At your service, Your Highness.

QUEEN LILIOSA

(*Without looking him*) Play me my favourite song before you fetch the champagne.

The butler crosses to a stereo in a corner of the lounge. He selects a CD and posts it into the stereo. Opera music fills the room. He walks stiffly towards the door. Exeunt IVANOV. *Alone,* QUEEN LILIOSA *rises and begins to waltz in the arms of an imaginary partner. After a while she dances caressing herself. Re-enter* IVANOV *with a bottle of wine and a glass on a tray, and stands still. She continues to dance in a provocative manner, her eyes closed.* IVANOV *coughs. She stops and faces him.*

Wow! Back already? You impress me with the almost military commitment you deliver your duties, Mr Ivanov. O! Caviare to the general!

IVANOV

(*Bows and smiles*)You are very generous with compliments, Queen Liliosa.

She crosses to him and picks the glass on the tray, turns and goes to the table.

QUEEN LILIOSA

(*Holding out the glass*) Come pour me a measure, Ivanov. The queen is instructing you.

IVANOV

I am sorry, Your Highness. Regulations say I should not stand too close to a queen.

QUEEN LILIOSA

(*With a hint of anger*) These regulations say you should disobey me –a queen? (*Solicitously*) Come pour me a measure of the champagne, Radimir Viktor Ivanov.

The queen holds out the glass, the butler in the backdrop and coming to her. He places the tray on the table, uncorks the bottle, stands about two paces from her and tries to fill her glass. She grabs his wrist and pulls him gently.

(*Seductively*) Be a man first, Mr Ivanov, a butler second. Do I scare you? I am a woman first, King Lima's eleventh wife second. I am like any other woman in Ngoloi. If cut, I bleed.

IVANOV

Your Highness, I must leave you alone now.

QUEEN LILIOSA

You only leave when I order you to. (*Squeezes his forearm*) My husband sent you to the London School of Butlers for a reason. He wanted the most refined butler. (*Sets the glass on the table*) You are exactly what he wanted –a gentleman exuding finesse in manner and in the delivery of his duties. There is an aristocratic air about you. (*Appraises him, fingering his shoulder and triceps, and gently lifting his chin*) You are *so-o* cultivated. No lady of substance would fail to admire you. (*Looks at the glass on the table*) Now pour me the champagne, my obedient servant.

IVANOV *pours a goblet in the glass, but she gulps it immediately and holds out the glass to him. He pours another measure. She gulps it and holds it out to him again. Shocked, he fills the glass to the brim. She sips leisurely.*

(*Erotically*) Listen to the music. It reaches for the soul and caresses it. Do you like it? Put the bottle down, Ivanov, and loosen up. You are not a Buddhist statue.

The queen pries the bottle from his hand and sets it on the table. She stands behind a stiff IVANOV, *stroking his shoulders, fingering his hair and sniffing his nape. The opera music continues to play.*

I miss the smell of a man. (*Sniffs him. Erotically*) There is a fire deep inside me not even the Tokyo Fire Department can put out. In the few instances the King tries to extinguish it, he is never man enough. He does it with haste... like a cockerel... like an amateur robbing a bank. (*Goes round and faces him*) Take me in your arms.

66

IVANOV

(*Crosses himself and clasps hands prayerfully*)Your Highness, I regard you with the utmost respect. I... I've a family and I love my wife. (*Retreats*) I can't do it. I – I – I am a baptised and confirmed Catholic. And it is Sunday –every Catholic altar is laden with appointments. Eucharist prayers are being offered to God.

She follows him, but IVANOV *continues to retreat until he stumbles into a sofa and sinks, his eyes riveted on the queen. She bores down on him, straddling him. The butler, too scared to touch her, slumps back.*

QUEEN LILIOSA

Imagine me an angel you've always desired. Kiss me now –like a gourmand munching a melon.

Her head slowly lowers towards his. They almost kiss, but IVANOV *turns his head.*

(*Irate, she grabs his shirt's labels*) Do you know what it means when you say: **At your service, Your Highness**? (*She gets off him and walks away. Disdainfully, looking away*) You are an inconsiderate animal, Ivanov. You've ashamed me beyond measure. Your punishment shall be as severe as a Siberian winter.

IVANOV

(*Apologetic, rising*) I beg you to forgive me, Your Highness.

QUEEN LILIOSA

(*Still looking away*) I am going to throw the towel away and bruise myself. Attempting to rape a queen could be punishable by death. Your wife shall find herself in my situation when you are gone. But unlike me, she shall chase demented paupers for it.

He crosses to her hesitantly. Standing behind her, he taps his hand on his thigh in a nervous byplay. Gingerly, he raises a hand and places it on her bare shoulder, both facing the same direction. She looks at the hand and delicately lays hers on top of his.

Call me Liliosa. But since you are about my father's age, call me your little swallowtail butterfly. Remove the towel. (*Turns around and faces him*)

They stare into each other's eyes. He places his hands on her shoulders.

Good, boy. I guessed a Russian would be expert at this. I heard that teetotaller Muscovites are endowed with Herculean stamina –that they are the strongest men in the world.

She kisses him with enthusiasm, unbuttons his shirt, removes and drops it. She holds his wrists and guides his hands to her back, her mouth coming to kiss his chest.

PM GAMATO (OFF-STAGE)

(*Booming*) Both king and commoner ought to see that trade winds are circumventing autocracy, a phenomenon that is creating black holes in every nation like ours. Black holes in space are spiralling vacuums. All vacuums are lifeless.

68

The queen quickly picks his shirt and stirs him out through a side door. Exeunt QUEEN LILIOSA *and* IVANOV. *Enter* KING LIMA *and* PM GAMATO, *the King's hands clasped behind his back. The Prime Minister is in an English suit, while the King is in a loose shirt and formal trousers. The King looks about, makes a face, crosses to switch the opera music off and sits in a chair by the table with newspapers.* PM GAMATO *sits in a sofa across the lounge. The King picks a newspaper from the pile and reads it quietly while the Prime Minister continues.*

Lion of Ngoloi, with all due respect, if you would stop overriding Parliament and the judiciary, and accord the Chief Justice freedom to perform his office, developed nations would fully recognise our Government.

KING LIMA
A load of codswallop! Who is the puppeteer, Prime Minister Gamato?

PM GAMATO
I am not a puppet, Your Majesty. I was elected.

KING LIMA
(*Throws away the paper*) Cut the nonsense, Prime Minister! You were elected because I tolerated democracy! I nominated you and influenced the electorate! Russians, Turks, Brazilians, Canadians, all have their own models of democracy.

PM GAMATO
Sir, flattery isn't my province. Your subjects live in squalor, which makes me Prime Minister to beggars, thieves

69

and roadside vegetable vendors. I can't hold my head high among other world leaders.

KING LIMA *turns, picks another newspaper and begins to read, seemingly not offended.*

Tourists come to gloat at our daughters' breasts. Lately the turnout was poor. Foreigners are beginning to see the wickedness of the whole thing.

The King folds the paper and puts it on the pile. One after the other, he picks the perfume and the bottle of lotion on the table, inspects, sets them down and picks the wineglass.

KING LIMA
(*Looking at a lipstick smudge on the glass*) I can hardly believe it. You – indigenous as I am – fighting our culture! (*Sets the glass down*)

PM GAMATO
The people have suffered enough. You dazzle them with bullet-proof limousines and luxury jets. When you suspect a cold, specialist doctors fly from Zurich to attend to you. Your wives shop alongside superstars and members of the British royal family.

KING LIMA
Taxpayers, I mean gravediggers and roadside vendors, buy you luxurious vehicles and pay your foreign holiday expenses. They put you in a mansion. If you aren't a white sepulchre, shouldn't you've demanded a meagre salary? (*Pauses*) I am cutting your remuneration by half with

immediate effect. The Government won't meet your holiday expenses anymore. (*Points at the exit*) You are not going to flog a dead horse.

The Prime Minister rises and walks slowly towards the exit.

This dynasty started in 1750 when your ancestors and mine were illiterate goats. Why should intellectualism control what wasn't founded on it?

At the exit, the Prime Minister turns and bows. Exeunt PM GAMATO. *The King angrily sweeps the pile of newspapers to the floor. Re-enter a sweating* IVANOV *carrying an orange drink, apples and a glass on a tray. His bowtie is askance, his shirt is not buttoned properly and the zip of his trousers is down. A flap of his shirt is poking through the open zip. The butler places the refreshments before the King and fills the glass. The servant's appearance disgusts the King.*

KING LIMA
You are sweating, Radimir Ivanov, and your zip is down.

IVANOV *gapes, looks at his zip and begins to correct the anomalies.*

IVANOV
I – I could be developing a fever, Sir. I suspect malaria.

KING LIMA
(*Pointing at the butler's zip*) If you are trying to charm the queens you are chasing the wind. My wives are beyond your league. (*Smiles*) And they are in the best hands.

IVANOV
Of course, Sir. (*Almost presentable now, bows*) My apologies, Sovereign.

KING LIMA
What are these doing here? (*Points at the wineglass and the perfume*) Who was drinking?

IVANOV
Her Highness, Queen Liliosa, Sir.

IVANOV *picks the newspapers on the floor and begins to arrange them neatly on the table again.*

KING LIMA
Radimir Ivanov, my priced Russian butler, you've lived in Africa for many years, but still you stand in the shadow of a ***Tamil Tiger*** and you can't see it.

IVANOV *shakes visibly.*

Go to any graveyard in the kingdom and see the evidence of what I mean. Why would a person of your intelligence toy with a killer responsible for the deaths of thousands? (*Pauses*) Olowolagba can always do your duties. Take two days off. Malaria can be deadly.

IVANOV
Thank you, Great Lion. You are most considerate.
Exeunt IVANOV *with the items. The King picks another newspaper and begins to browse it.*
Curtain

Scene Two

Same morning
A private posh bedroom

[Act 4]

QUEEN TIAFORA *and* RAJ GOPAL *are fondling each other propped up on a headboard; she is sitting between his legs, both facing the same direction. A sheet covers them and a crumbled one is at their feet. On a bedside table are two cocktails and an almost empty champagne bottle. The couple's shoes, clothes and the queen's undergarments are strewn on the floor. Classic instrumental Indian music is playing.*

QUEEN TIAFORA

I want to be with you forever, but not in this godforsaken kingdom.

RAJ GOPAL

Be patient, dear. I was at the British Embassy on Friday. The visas weren't out yet, dear.

QUEEN TIAFORA

I told you to grease the officials' palms. Do you really want to live with me abroad?

RAJ GOPAL

Be patient, sweetheart. It's difficult to bribe British officials. Tomorrow I'll push further.

QUEEN TIAFORA

O! How I longed to be in your arms again. O! How I lust to be in them forever. Perhaps only then will I see the colour of love for the first time. Poets suggest it has different shades of pink, but I am yet to see it.

RAJ GOPAL

(*Toying with her hair*) A splendid life awaits you in Scotland –the paradise of the birch, the elm and the blackthorn. Lima's henchmen and scouts will look for you on every continent. I bought a castle in Edinburgh. When your disappearance ceases to be news, I'll marry you in a Hindu temple along the River Ganges. The gods are ready to bless us.

Enter JEFFERSON *in a balaclava mask, his pistol leading. The lovebirds freeze.*

JEFFERSON

Mr Raj Gopal – the banker – the third richest man in Ngoloi. (*Closes the door and walks to a chair in a corner*) Of course, the Great Lion is the richest man in the land. You inherited a vast fortune from your father, an alms giver. (*Sits, the pistol trained at the lovers*) He was fearful of all Hindu gods. Mr Gupta Gopal washed the feet of orphans and widows. He distanced himself from married women.

RAJ GOPAL

You are frightening us. Who are you? Please tell us what you want.

JEFFERSON

(*Crosses his legs*) You live in a Malibu-style mansion with your family. This must be a love nest. What are you doing in bed with His Majesty's wife on a Sunday?

RAJ GOPAL

I am sorry, sir, but love is always beyond human logic. Lord Shiva my witness, I am not a poacher by nature. There were times when I thought she was my soul mate. Now I see I deluded myself. I'll perform ablution for my sin.

JEFFERSON *removes the mask and drops it.*

QUEEN TIAFORA

(*Quietly, touching her mouth*) Jeff... you followed me?

JEFFERSON

Lately I was asked to watch you, Your Highness. But I never thought I would see you in such a compromising position.

QUEEN TIAFORA

We can talk, Jeff. Let's talk.

JEFFERSON

What is your proposal, Your Highness?

RAJ GOPAL

I've twenty-thousand US dollars in the house, and some polished diamonds. There is a safe over there. (*Points to a corner*)

JEFFERSON *motions him to go to fetch the fortune.* RAJ GOPAL, *in a beach short, leaves the bed and crosses to a safe in a corner. He unlocks the safe and begins taking out wads of US dollars and placing them on the floor.*

JEFFERSON
(*Watching him unpack the safe*) There is something interesting about money, Mr Gopal. I've lived long enough in Africa to think like a Bantu. Benjamin Franklin is on the money you are emptying out because he was a statesman, an inventor and a diplomat. I would resort to **hari-kari** if I learned the man touched other people's wives. The statesman must be turning in his tomb as I speak.

A pile of US dollars on the floor, the safe empty, GOPAL *straightens and hands* JEFFERSON *a tied hessian sachet. The henchman beckons him back with the pistol, steps back, dips his free hand into the sachet, inspects some diamonds, puts them back in the container and pockets it.*

Yet there is something even more interesting about money, Mr Gopal. Jesus knew where every coin was. Judas, his appointed treasurer, was bought with the Saviour's pieces of silver. I am neither Hindu nor Sikh, but I've come to believe that everything belongs to God –including the Devil.

QUEEN TIAFORA
(*Pleading*) You got the diamonds and the money, what more do you want?

JEFFERSON

(*Stepping towards the Indian*) I don't keep my word, Your Highness. There is no aorta of nobility in my blood. My father was a libidinous tramp in the Docklands of London, so I heard. He never married my mother, a cocaine-addicted whore who took her life at the age of twenty-one, when I was three —so I also heard. (*Presses the muzzle behind Gopal's ear*) Don't worry. I've done this before. You won't feel a thing.

QUEEN TIAFORA

Jeff, you are a mercenary, or thereabouts near that category. The diamonds are worth over a hundred thousand dollars. Take your riches and go.

JEFFERSON

In some countries, adulterers are stoned on the spot. There is something so disgustingly wrong about adultery that an ungifted carnal man like me finds inexplicable. You are asking me for any colour so long as it's black.

QUEEN TIAFORA *wraps herself in the bed sheet and leaves the bed, the linen tacked under her armpits.*

Why do you cover yourself? Your Highness, nothing on your body can arrest my eyes.

QUEEN TIAFORA

(*Rooted, clipping the sheet under her armpits*) How would murder benefit you, Jefferson? God's tenets are not your province. Gays were never called. Mr Gopal and I intend to run. He can appropriate an eighth of his wealth to you, which should rest the matter. Let him put it down in an affidavit.

JEFFERSON

(*Laughs briefly*) Queen Tiafora, I am as gay as many bishops, archbishops and cardinals in the world. Do you know the reason God tested Abraham? So that the world would know that no one is allowed to kill in the name of religion. But now I must kill both of you so that you know that God also inspires gays, ghouls and goblins.

Cautiously, the pistol still pressed on the Indian's head, he reaches for the crumbled sheet on the bed and throws it at the queen who grabs it. He beckons her to him, steps aside, motions her to stand beside the Indian and gestures that they drape themselves in the linen. The two hold hands and comply; standing blindly under the sheet, only their legs showing.

This room is Spartan. We don't want to mess it. You'll walk to the bathroom. Pray that I experience an angelic visitation along the way so that you might live. Walk.

The couple hesitates, turns and walks timidly towards a door, bumps into a wall, gropes, finds the door's handle and opens it. Still holding hands, they exeunt into a passage. JEFFERSON remains rooted, the pistol trained at them off-stage. He fires several times into the passage amid brief screams from the two, blows smoke from the muzzle and stares at the stack of money on the floor. Shortly, a blood-stained RAJ GOPAL staggers back into the bedroom and drops dead. The queen's screams resume in the passage and transform to heavy panting.

(*To the passage*) Get up and cover your nudity. You are not hit, Tiafora. You'll tell others the lesson in Abraham's sacrifice, but you are not returning to the palace. By nightfall tomorrow you shall be forever out of my sight or you are either dead or in jail. A seminal odour on you tells me traces of adultery can still be extracted from your body forty-eight hours from now. You talked about Scotland —to that country you'll go. Your airfare is in the loot on the floor. With your Khoi-San hips, I bet you could start a thriving brothel in exile. This is a gay man's gift of life to an adulteress. Come and fetch your clothes.

Re-enter a shaky, teary QUEEN TIAFORA *covering herself with a bloodied sheet. She goes round picking her clothes, the henchman's pistol trained at her.*

Curtain

Scene Three

Monday morning
A palatial study

[Act 4]

KING LIMA, *casually dressed, is at a shelf searching for a book. Enter* OLOWOLAGBA *ushering* PROF PITONI *in a business suit and bearing his briefcase. Both bow in unison. Exeunt* OLOWOLAGBA. *The professor remains rooted, frightened.*

KING LIMA

(*Gesturing to a chair*)Tell me the good news. Today is Monday. Is he dead?

The professor sits in the chair, sets his briefcase down and shakes his head.

You see... Katomene Hasa wants to be like Che Guevara...like Patrice Lumumba...like Steve Biko.... like Ken Saro-Wiwa. Why do you deny him the chance? Kill him.

PROF PITONI

Jefferson's hands were full lately. I am sure you've heard about the banishment of Queen Tiafora and the death of Mr Gopal, the businessman.

KING LIMA

Jefferson took care of the matter yesterday. (*Browsing a book*) Tiafora won't be mentioned near me again. Intelligence said she was holed at the British ambassador's residence awaiting her visa. Gopal's body was taken to Herr Hoffmann and his son. What brings you here, Prof Pitoni?

PROF PITONI
Sir, I saw the *Sangoma* leaving Katomene's house on Saturday night.

KING LIMA
(*Ponders for a moment*) Liquidate her. The Hoffmanns need more human fodder.

PROF PITONI
It's unheard of to kill a *sangoma*! No one wants to horde all the evil spirits on earth.

KING LIMA
(*Shelves the book and sits behind a desk*) The Hoffmanns are as important as Death. Would you like to die in her place, Prof Pitoni?

PROF PITONI
Sovereign, with all due respect, Jesus did that perfectly for everybody.

KING LIMA
(*Smiles*) O! An envoy of the Pope! Clearly, you are in the wrong profession, Uncle. Place an advertisement in the newspapers for your understudy —an astute, non-assumptive and non-compromising, robust African, someone who can use an arrow and an automatic pistol at the same time.

PROF PITONI

I think you misunderstood me, Your Majesty. It takes a more fearsome witch-doctor to kill a witch-doctor.

KING LIMA

(*Harshly*) Be the *more* fearsome *Sangoma*! What brings you here?

PROF PITONI

We once had *tête-à-tête*. Your favourite bagpipe band was the subject. You impressed it on me that you found its mace-bearer irresistibly petite. As a result, you promised her and the band study scholarships at the University of St Andrews, in Scotland.

KING LIMA

(*Demurs, thoughtful*) I remember clearly. It was at the beginning of the year. (*Annoyed*) I thought she would take part in the Reed Dance. It appears Scottish values have crept into the girl. What did you gather?

PROF PITONI

Her name is Mimudeh, a Forth Form student at Oro High School. She is sixteen and the brightest girl among her school peers.

KING LIMA

Tell me more. Is she a Hermann Gmeiner orphan? Does she have parents and a lineage?

PROF PITONI

Her mother is an accountant in a non-governmental organisation that deals with children's rights. Her father, you won't believe it, is this troublesome legislator–Katomene Hasa.

KING LIMA

Neither the Euphrates nor the Amazon can stand between the Lion and his desires. Abduct the girl!

PROF PITONI

My God! We cannot do that. It's a quantum leap to the Stone Age.

KING LIMA

In many developed countries girls of twelve can consent to sex. In the Middle East they consider the onset of puberty. Mimudeh is sixteen, if I may just refresh your memory.

PROF PITONI

Lion of Ngoloi, foreigners are not our mentors.

KING LIMA

Prof Pitoni, our clothes and ideals are European. Our Parliament is English. Our legislators move motions and debate in English. Our law is Roman-Dutch. Learned one, defy the Lion at your own risk. This is your final warning. See yourself out.

The professor rises and walks towards the exit. Exeunt PROF PITONI.

Curtain

Act Five

Lunch Hour, Tuesday
A footpath in a flowery public park

Elegantly uniformed students from Oro High, some chattering, some in pairs, some playful, are trickling homeward. TWO WOMEN *in headscarves and carrying big handbags, apparently Jehovah's Witnesses, are trying in vain to hand out biblical leaflets to the students. Off-stage emanates city noise; hooting cars, barking dogs, yelling fruit vendors and beggars, etc. The one-directional flow quickly fades and the women sit on a park bench.*

ARCHER' VOICE (OFF-STAGE**)**
(Booming and Thespian)
Why come provocatively dressed like this?
I sniff a scandal in the making, but at your age
I read you like unadorned Stone Age calligraphy.
Capture the created image and its offence:
The timing, the scene and the pornography
Of a priest in his underclothes set to retire,
Alone with a schoolgirl in nightclub attire,
It's late at night and the two are in his bedroom.
We're like two lovers in a dacha on a lonely shore.
Surely someone desires to see me pulling a rickshaw.

Enter MIMUDEH, *looking at a page in an open copy of* **Shrouded Blessings**, *followed by* ARCHER, *both are in Oro school uniform and also homeward bound. The boy is carrying Mimudeh's loaded satchel and his.*

MIMUDEH

Wow! That was Father Flynn pleading with Naomi, the seductress. And you recited the passage with an astronomical precision. Now I see why you attained a distinction. (*Challenged, gives him the book*) I am fond of the priest's last words in Act Three, Scene Three.

Both stop.

ARCHER

(*Flips through the book, opens a page and stares at it*) I am there, girlfriend. What does the father say?

MIMUDEH

(*Crosses herself and recites in a feigned masculine voice*)
Open your eyes and see the falsity of the mirage.
The tumultuous Red Sea hid a passage.
Sweetness hid in the bitter water at Mara.
Daily for forty years Israel was bitten.
Daily for forty years the House of Israel was smitten.
Of creation is it not written:
Out of darkness light came out?

ARCHER

Mimudeh, the Scottish bursary is yours! I foresee you landing at Glasgow International Airport. Should you choose; you might end up a Supreme Court judge in Scotland. (*Dramatically bows to her*) The Honourable Lord Mimudeh McLeod, My Lord. (*Bowed, gives her the book*)

MIMUDEH

(*In mock frustration*) Is that all Her Lordship Mimudeh McLeod could expect from her most obedient and humble servant, Dr Archer McLeod? This day, Tuesday the tenth of September, I hereby find you guilty and order you to kiss Her Lordship this instant. (*Leans forward, pouts her lips and closes her eyes*)

ARCHER

Mimudeh! You are demanding a kiss in public?

MIMUDEH

(*Still posed for the kiss*) Be quick, Archer. My mother's car is idling outside this park. She'll come looking for me at any moment now.

He looks about and gives her a snap kiss. Both sigh simultaneously, exaggeratedly satisfied, touching their chests. The TWO WOMEN *rise from the bench and approach them, one is holding out colourful leaflets and a Bible, the other has leaflets and her handbag is open. The Bible bearer opens the book and approaches* ARCHER *as if to show him a passage, while the second one advances to* MIMUDEH. *As* ARCHER *looks at the woman and her open Bible, he turns his back to* MIMUDEH *who is suddenly engulfed in a cloud of chalky plumes squeezed from the handbag.*

MIMUDEH *screams, shutting her eyes and drops the book. Shocked and puzzled, the boy turns and looks at her. The woman's handbag is now closed and held behind the woman's back while she is holding out the leaflets to the girl.* MIMUDEH *gasps, staggering from the woman, coughing several times and clutching her neck, her eyes vacant.*

ARCHER

Hey! What is it? What's happening? (*Breaks her fall and gently lowers her to the ground*)

The girl lies prone. He puts the satchels down and, squatting besides her, stares at her and then at the women.

1ˢᵀ WOMAN (BIBLE BEARER)

(*Aghast and pressing a handkerchief to her nose*) Must be an asthmatic attack! Or is it a heart-attack?

2ᴺᴰ WOMAN

(*Retreating and also holding a handkerchief against her nose*) Somebody call 911!

ARCHER

(*Kneeling beside Mimudeh, panicking and clumsily at First Aid*) She's breathing! Her mother is outside the park! (*Rises*) Mrs Hasa can take her to hospital.

1ˢᵀ WOMAN

Thank God. Please inform her immediately. Every minute counts.

Exeunt ARCHER running; without the satchels and the book. The TWO WOMEN look about and dash to the schoolgirl as they draw a large shawl, Cordoba hat and dark glasses from their handbags. Squatting and covering her torso with the shawl, they quickly fit the hat and the glasses on MIMUDEH and whisk her off-stage in the opposite direction the boy took.

Final curtain

Afterword

This play was inspired by the following reports:

Miss Zena Mahlangu, a student, was picked from her school by two female courtiers two weeks ago and taken to the numerous royal lodges in and around Mbabane (Swaziland) to undergo the elaborate training to become a royal bride....

-The British Telegraph & The BBC, October, 2002

Swaziland's autocratic King Mswati III has obtained a private jet, despite the majority of his countrymen continuing to live in abject poverty....

-Sunday Times (South Africa), April 29, 2012

Book II

Square Circle In A Triangle

Success is founded on conquest.
Darkness delivered light.
Setbacks shroud opportunities.
Sons and daughters, remember this always.
Áaýw^t&u#hl=b^m&týu^Álu!m=z=B!yj&a#rvÁaý!t*G#hl#u+r`w=t;*+*
.u*wyl
Ex 20:26

None are more hopelessly enslaved than those who
falsely believe they are free.
-Johann Wolfgang von Goethe
German poet, 1749 - 1832

Characters

King Lima III, *King of Ngoloi (±45 yrs)*
Queen Mother Jirimita, *The King's Mother*
Queen Jolina, *The King's 8th Wife*
Prof Pitoni, *A Royal Political Advisor*
Chuchu, *A Royal Diviner (*Sangoma, *Female)*
Radimir Ivanov *(White)*, *A Royal Butler (±48 yrs)*
Jefferson Buckley *(White)*, *A Henchman (40s)*
Jervaulx Olowolagba *(Dwarf)*, *A Royal Orderly*
Pm Ete Gamato, *Prime Minister*
Katomene Hasa, *A Member of Parliament (Early 40s)*
Belemina, *Katomene's Wife*
Mimudeh, *Katomene's Daughter (16 yrs)*
Yemudeh, *Mimudeh's Identical Twin*
Archer McLeod *(White)*, *Mimudeh's Boyfriend (18 yrs)*
Spencer, *Archer's Father*
Laura, *Archer's Mother*
Bishop Hasbrouck *(White)*, *A Catholic Bishop*
Father Tito, *A Catholic Abbot*
Gen. Okata Ofuji, *An army Commander-General*
Dr Fong Cheng *(Chinese Male)*, *Company President*
Dr Shin Lin *(Chinese Female)*, *Company Chairwoman*
Sgt Gopo, *A Police Sergeant*
Dr Sada, *A Police Psychologist*
Dr Dickson *(White)*, *A Medical Doctor*
Two Women

Plus:
Justice Ishmael Mila, *A High Court Judge*
Adv. Mbani, *An Advocate At Law*

Four Firemen
Two Policemen
Two Paramedics
A Limp "Patient"

Act One

Scene One

Afternoon
A torture chamber

JEFFERSON *is standing at a weaponry rack in a corner. It holds long pokers, hooks, tongs, and machetes of different makes. He selects a machete and fingers its cutting edge as he walks towards a noose suspended from the roof; below which is a vacant chair. A spotlight in the ceiling is focused on a blindfolded, school-uniformed* MIMUDEH *bound to another chair. She struggles mildly and snivels. He crosses to her, his face grave, squats and removes the blindfold. She blinks several times, looking about.*

JEFFERSON

(*Fingering her cheeks*) If you don't cooperate you make it perilous for yourself. I would hate to kill a bright girl like you. (*Holds her chin, and brings his face close to hers*) But should you choose death, my hand will not tremble. (*Stands erect and paces*) In case you are disoriented —it's Tuesday the tenth of September. Your name is Mimudeh Hasa. Your father is Hon. Katomene Hasa. The Reed Dance ended a week ago. The fluffs of the bishop bird are still settling.

MIMUDEH

(*Sobbing*) I know who I am. Where am I? What do you want me to do? (*Screams, struggling to free herself*) Mammy! Daddy! Somebody help me!

JEFFERSON

(*Parodying sarcastically louder*) **Somebody help me**! (*Laughs*) This chamber is soundproof. Welcome to Heaven or Hell, depending on what you choose. It would be diabolic of you to do injustice to yourself by not cooperating. (*Pauses*) He begs your hand in marriage.

MIMUDEH

What're you talking about? Who?

JEFFERSON

Who else besides His Majesty, the Lion of Ngoloi?

MIMUDEH

(*Slowly in disbelief and fear*) King Lima? Why me? This must be a mistake.

JEFFERSON

(*Pacing*) Fortune knocks at your door and you ask: **Why me**? Perhaps you've hidden charms only the royal eye could see. (*Surveying her*) Young as you are, yet to display all your fruits, you have captured the King's eye. (*Holds the machete upright like a drum major's mace and marches momentarily*) You'll love him and dance for him some more in the privacy of this palace. If you married him the Reed Dance wouldn't be held again. You shall lead a life of gracious etiquette.

MIMUDEH

(*Teary*) I'll never love him, not even in a thousand and one years.

JEFFERSON

At sixteen, you are probably too young to understand these things, exactly why you had to be kidnapped, exactly why you should be killed if you turned him down. (*Solicitously*) Step into a new world of silver and gold far from the haunts of ordinary men. Your dad will be proud of you. Wealth shall flow like the Nile into your father's hands.

MIMUDEH

Doesn't this uniform mean anything to you?

JEFFERSON

O! I see now that talk about your brilliance was assumptive. (*Returns the machete to the rack, draws a slender dagger, crosses to her, kneels and peers into her face menacingly*) Here time is always a premium; therefore I won't try to convince you. (*Slides the tip of the dagger into her nostril*) Be careful now, burning pansy butterfly. Sudden movements could see you lose your nose or an eye, prematurely. I've seen it happen in this chamber. (*Pokes inside her nostril; drawing a rivulet of blood*) You chose death.

MIMUDEH *sobs, grunting, holding her head still.*

Soon you shall be among angels in Heaven, my dear. Do you've a boyfriend? How I wish he could see this. (*Manically*) Romeo! Romeo! Juliet is bleeding!

Enter OLOWOLAGBA *bearing a large banquet of red roses and a covered serving tray.* JEFFERSON *turns the other lights in the chamber on, fully revealing the racked weapons and blood-stained walls as the dwarf places the flowers and the tray before her.* JEFFERSON *returns the dagger to the rack and stands in a corner as* OLOWOLAGBA *appraises a bloodied* MIMUDEH.

OLOWOLAGBA

The peace of God be with you, my daughter. My name is Mr Jervaulx Olowolagba. But you'll call me Father Olowolagba; for it is the affectionate one –high sounding but with little relevance. I cherish my first name – Jervaulx. English missionaries in Lagos named me after a twelfth century Cistercian monastery in Wensleydale, England. It made me a Christian from the cradle. Our clan only serves kings and noblemen. That is how I found work with His Majesty, but as an orderly. But often I serve as a priest by choice. (*Stooping, he uncovers the tray, places the flowers on her lap and stands erect*) His Majesty sends you these delicacies. You shall feed the temple of God now, my daughter, as a duty to your Creator. The King himself handpicked the roses. (*Nods at Jefferson*)

JEFFERSON *leaves the corner.* OLOWOLAGBA *and he begin untying the girl, her wrists first.*

MIMUDEH

(*Being untied, crying*) I can't... I can't love or marry a man with thirteen wives. O! This is a nightmare. I'll wake up from it.

OLOWOLAGBA

(*Untying her*) Love has nothing to do with it. None of his wives loves him. It's about wealth – overwhelming wealth.

MIMUDEH

(*Shocked*) What business have I listening to you? I am not going to marry him! Kill me! Kill me now! Cut me into a hundred pieces!

The men drop the ropes and stand in front of her.

OLOWOLAGBA

O! Is it not written: **what man is there of you, whom of his son ask a fish, will he give him a serpent?** Though I am a staunch believer of Mathew, I remain Igbo. The Igbo are genteel by nature —they don't pester.

The dwarf makes a cut-throat gesture at JEFFERSON. *The henchman crosses to the rack, picks a serrated machete and comes to stand behind* MIMUDEH. *Crossing himself solemnly,* OLOWOLAGBA *retreats.*

MIMUDEH

(*Casts the roses away and lowers her head; exposing her neck*) There is my neck! Cut it!

OLOWOLAGBA

Aren't you going to say a prayer? The Lord's Prayer could be a good send-off.

MIMUDEH

That is a matter between me and my God. Do it, I command you!

Behind her, JEFFERSON *raises the machete.*

OLOWOLAGBA

Haven't you got any last words?

MIMUDEH

I've already said them.

With his other hand, JEFFERSON *rubs the girl's neck gently, the machete still raised.*

OLOWOLAGBA

You'll go straight to Heaven; God loves children. (*Heavenwards*) Accept her soul. Forgive her her trespasses.

MIMUDEH

You are giving me a serpent. Do it now!

JEFFERSON *decides to saw the girl's head off and places the blade against her larynx. The orderly looks away as he applies pressure.* MIMUDEH *makes an agonised face. Blood trickles down the blade. She holds the blade, which cuts her palms, and she screams. The door flings open. Enter* QUEEN JOLINA *in a long dress and a matching, towering headscarf.*

QUEEN JOLINA

(*Hands on her bosom, shocked*) Geez! Put that machete down, I order you!

JEFFERSON *lowers the machete. Crying,* MIMUDEH *inspects her injured palms and clutches her neck.*

JEFFERSON

(*Bows*) Your Highness, I am a tool in His Majesty's hands.

QUEEN JOLINA

Drop the machete, Jeff! Drop it now!

JEFFERSON *stares at* QUEEN JOLINA, *drops the machete and retreats.*

(*To the orderly*) Olo, you know every scripture in the Bible, when are you going to observe its tenets?

OLOWOLAGBA

(*Bows*) Your Highness, it is pagan to execute people without giving them a chance to repent or to learn the opinion of God. Is it not written: *My people are destroyed for lack of knowledge?*

QUEEN JOLINA

I suspected something was wrong when I saw you with the roses and taking the opposite direction to Queen Ayola's quarters. I followed you to satisfy my curiosity because there is no shade of romance elsewhere in this palace. (*Pauses*) I don't care about your instructions. Take the girl to the guest wing. She is now my guest.

The men bow and begin preparations to evacuate MIMUDEH, *the queen watching.*

Curtain

Scene Two

Afternoon
The legislator's lounge-cum-dining room

[Act 1]

BELEMINA, *sobbing quietly, and* KATOMENE *are huddled in a sofa.* ARCHER, *in school uniform,* SPENCER *and* LAURA McLEOD *are sitting across the Hasas, watching them pensively. A portable radio on a coffee table before them is giving the news:*

FEMININE VOICE (RADIO)

In a movie-style kidnapping that shocked members of the public at Oro High School at about 1 pm yesterday, Mimudeh Hasa, a Fourth Form student, was kidnapped as she left school. The sixteen-year old girl was kidnapped by two women in headscarves after she fell unconscious under unclear circumstances, according to an eye-witness, one Archer McLeod, a friend and schoolmate of the victim.

BELEMINA *sobs inconsolably.* KATOMENE *mutely tries to calm her. The* McLEODS *are at a loss. The radio news continues:*

It is said the schoolgirl collapsed under unclear circumstances when the two women approached Mimudeh and the witness as the students were walking through Totororo Park, which is adjacent to Oro High School. Since the victim's mother, Mrs Belemina Hasa, was waiting to pick her daughter outside the park, the witness rushed to inform her about the incidence, but he

103

and the mother found Mimudeh and the two women missing only a few minutes later. The police have since established that the two women were bogus evangelists.

Investigations are still at a preliminary stage, but Mimudeh's father, Hon. Katomene Hasa, has already indicated that the family will reward anyone who comes forward with information that will lead to the recovery of their daughter. Members of the public with information are encouraged to make use of the police's hotlines, suggestion boxes or may visit their nearest police station.

Meanwhile, a cross section of the society, including teachers and fellow students at the school, has condemned the kidnapping in the strongest terms. People described the perpetrators as barbaric, heartless and subhuman. Members of the public are warned against approaching the criminals should they be sighted as they are potentially dangerous. That ends the news.

KATOMENE *leans forward, switches the radio off and stares quizzically at* SPENCER.

SPENCER
I don't know what to think, but there are many possibilities.

KATOMENE
What do you suspect, Eng. McLeod?

SPENCER

I don't want to knock the breath out of you, Hon. Hasa and Mrs Hasa.

KATOMENE

Be ruthless, Engineer, I beg you. Tell us what instinct is saying to you.

SPENCER

That she was kidnapped for ransom cannot be ruled out, Hon. Hasa. I also suspect human or body-part trafficking. The religious element of the women could be indicative of voodooists. Everything is still mysterious at the moment. If she's alive we expect her kidnappers to make contact.

The doorbell rings. KATOMENE *rises and crosses to take it. Enter* BISHOP HASBROUCK, *in a purple skullcap, and* FATHER TITO, *both in a dark suits. The abbot is carrying a small suitcase and draping a white robe over his left hand. Everyone rises and shakes the hands of the newcomers. All sit except the new arrivals.* FATHER TITO *places the suitcase in front of the priest and opens it. The suitcase has vestments and silver appointments; priestly robes, crucifixes, including a seven-stick candle holder, and a bottle of altar wine. The abbot genuflects, dons the white robe over his clothes and crosses himself. He begins handing the bishop his garments in an attitude of supplication.*

BISHOP HASBROUCK

I came as soon as I heard the news. (*Donning his priestly robes over his suit*) The Devil is a liar and a trickster. The Psalmist says: **He shall cover thee with his feathers, and under his wings shalt thou trust**. The hand of God shall

105

hover over Mimudeh. Only good shall come out of her disappearance. (*Now in colourful robes, he genuflects thrice and launches into rites, his voice sangfroid*) I believe in the Holy Spirit, the holy Catholic Church, the communion of saints, the forgiveness of sins, the resurrection of the body, and the life everlasting. Peace be with you.

ALL
And also with you.

The abbot puts the wireless radio under the coffee table and sets the chalice, wine bottle and candle-holder on the table, inserts seven candle sticks into the holder, lights them and pours a small measure of wine into the chalice. He crosses himself, retreats to a sofa and sits.

BISHOP HASBROUCK
(*Crosses himself and raises the chalice*) Blessed are you, Lord, God of all creation. Through Your goodness we have this wine to offer, fruit of the vine and work of human hands. It'll become our spiritual drink. (*Lowers the chalice down*) Pray, brethren, that our sacrifice may be acceptable to God, the almighty Father.

ALL
May the Lord accept the sacrifice at your hands for the praise and glory of His name, for our good, and the good of all His Church.

All pray silently, momentarily, heads bowed.

BISHOP HASBROUCK
For Mimudeh Hasa, lift up your hearts to the Lord.

ALL

We lift them up to the Lord.

BISHOP HASBROUCK

Let us give thanks to the Lord our God.

ALL

It is right to give Him thanks and praise.

The bishop sips from the chalice and crosses to the abbot who rises, crosses himself again and sips from it in the hands of his senior. KATOMENE and BELEMINA rise. The McLEODS exchange glances and rise too. The senior priest turns and approaches the communion recipients in the following order: KATOMENE, BELEMINA, SPENCER, LAURA and then ARCHER. They all cross themselves and sit as soon as they partake. The abbot receives the empty chalice from the bishop, sets it on the coffee table and stands aside, his hands clasped.

BISHOP HASBROUCK

The impromptu Mass for Mimudeh Hasa is ended, let us wait in peace.

ALL

Thanks be to God.

The priests cross themselves and begin removing their vestments.

KATOMENE

Your Lordship, I believe the kidnapper is someone we know.

BISHOP HASBROUCK

(*Removing the vestments and folding them. Sternly*) We believe in Jesus Christ. He was born of the Virgin Mary, and became man. He suffered under Pontius Pilate. He'll come again to judge the living and the dead.

All nod and cross themselves.

Curtain

Scene Three

Morning
A palatial bedroom

[Act 1]

In the room with fresh garlands, MIMUDEH *is sitting on a stool and* QUEEN JOLINA, *in a different set of matching attire including a headscarf, is on another. The schoolgirl has just bathed; her skin is oiled. White towels are wound around her hair and body. The queen is bandaging the girl's right hand. Her left hand is already dressed. An Elastoplasts bandage is below the girl's larynx. A first-aid kit lies open at their feet.*

QUEEN JOLINA

(*Dressing the girl's right hand*) Thank God only the skin was cut. Were it not for my curiosity yesterday, they would've killed you. (*Paradoxically*) I am his eldest wife. We have been married for over twenty-five years now. He looked at me with admiration only for the first few months after the Reed Dance. Tourists came in droves to witness my selection. The fanfare was great and humbling. But it's all gone now. Here am I, sad in a splendid palace, sobbing among roses in full bloom. (*Through with dressing her hand, she rises, crosses to a window and speaks looking out the window*) No difference exists between me and a palace ornament – a vase or a wall hanging. I feel like an artefact he bought in a curio shop. (*Sighs*) Even when you are with him, he is never there. It's ironic that this villa was an elite brothel before the royal family bought it. (*Turns and faces the girl*) I must convince you to marry him, or you are dead. Though I am the Queen of Queens, I am a prisoner

109

here. I hardly leave this palace unless he grants me permission, yet I remain his wife. Queen Tiafora shall never be seen again for daring to sneak out of the palace. A reliable source informed me she collected her passport and British visa on Monday. I pray she's alive and well somewhere in Britain.

MIMUDEH
How about my education? What about my dreams?

QUEEN JOLINA
What did you want to become... a criminal lawyer, an aerodynamics engineer, a paediatric oncologist? If you insist the King can send you to the best colleges in Britain or America.

Enter QUEEN MOTHER JIRIMITA *in a floor-sweeping, majestic dress. She is holding a pair of binoculars.*

QUEEN MOTHER JIRIMITA
(*Walking into the bedroom*) For some reason the word **thallium** came into my head when Jefferson and Olo told me you took the girl yesterday. Doctors say the poison is usually hard to detect until its victim is comatose or dead. What're you discussing with the girl? Were you authorised to talk to her?

QUEEN JOLINA
(*Curtsies and assumes a posture of utmost respect. Head bowed*) Queen Mother, their methods were ammoniac. The girl is still young and timid, and in matters of life and substance, void. I

thought a word with her would bring the eventual good His Majesty sought.

QUEEN MOTHER JIRIMITA
(*Stands in the middle of the room and ponders for a moment*) They told me the girl was intelligent. No one should vest too much time persuading her. A girl of her IQ knows the difference between Paradise and Hell. Whatever she chooses; we must all know it's a well-considered choice.

QUEEN JOLINA
(*Head still bowed*) Absolutely, Queen Mother. Allow me to leave her in your good hands.

The queen walks towards the exit. Exeunt QUEEN JOLINA.

QUEEN MOTHER JIRIMITA
It's time to say goodbye to your schoolgirl mentality. Imagine a romantic honeymoon on the French or Italian Riviera. Already I can hear Italian violinists playing a love song at your wedding. (*Crosses to* MIMUDEH *and gives her the pair of binoculars. She points to a different window*) Could you look out that window, my dear?

Confounded, the girl hesitates, then rises and goes to the window, draws a curtain aside and looks out, her back to the queen.

What do you see?

MIMUDEH
Flower gardens... a sky full of tumultuous clouds.
QUEEN MOTHER JIRIMITA

111

There is some activity going on beyond the gardens. Use the pair of binoculars.

MIMUDEH *looks at her bandaged hands, picks the binoculars and looks through them.*

MIMUDEH
(*Looking through the binoculars*) I see two white men dressed like garbage men or... eh... like mortuary attendants. One is elderly, the other is young. They are on the premises but far from the palace.

QUEEN MOTHER JIRIMITA
Are they picnicking? Are they picking Floribundas? What're they doing, Mimudeh?

MIMUDEH
(*Looking out through the binoculars*) The pair is arranging a cleaver, a chopper, a four-pound hammer, pliers and a chainsaw on a stainless steel table. Something like a sausage machine is mounted on the table. The table is near a pit and a large basin, or is it a bathtub?

QUEEN MOTHER JIRIMITA
Go on, my dear. Tell me all that you see.

MIMUDEH
The men are standing in a semi-erected camping tent. The tent is still under pitching around the pit, the table and the bathtub. But the roof is already in place.

QUEEN MOTHER JIRIMITA

That is Herr Dietrich Hoffmann, or Mr Dietrich Hoffmann, and his son, Heinrich. The Lion picked them from Totororo Park. They were hand-to-mouth vagrants – perhaps fugitives who fled Germany but failed to make it here. What is happening now?

MIMUDEH
(*Looking through the binoculars*) The son –Heinrich, you said – is now testing the chainsaw.

Chainsaw noise emanates momentarily from a distance outside the bedroom.

He has set it on the table, but Mr Hoffmann has lifted a flap of the tent. My view is blocked now.

QUEEN MOTHER JIRIMITA
You can put the binoculars down. What you've just seen is neither a puzzle nor a *Nō* –a Japanese play with a symbolic meaning.

MIMUDEH *sets the binoculars on the sill, turns and faces the queen with a puzzled look.*

The Hoffmanns quarter human remains. They then chop the quarters and sort of grate the pieces into pulp. They submerge the pulp into an acid bath. Whatever withstands their nitric acid, they cremate in the basin you saw. Most of the staff here have been granted a day off. That is the custom here every time Herr Hoffmann and Heinrich are invited. (*Pauses*) But we have never called them in September, especially nine days after the Reed Dance. I don't think they like their job, but it has given them dignity and luxury. Don't worry, Mimudeh. My son will find another girl – perhaps someone younger and prettier, but wise as the Hoffmanns. He'll stand on your ashes and exchange marriage vows with his sweetheart.

MIMUDEH *gapes, leans on the wall, slides to the floor and sits dejectedly with her knees propped up.*

Curtain

Act Two

Scene One

Night
A palatial office

KING LIMA, *dressed in distinct African attire, is playing chess alone behind a grandiose desk. The office is decorated with effigies, flowers, the King's portraits and the nation's flag. Large relief maps are on the walls. Enter* OLOWOLAGBA *and bows.*

OLOWOLAGBA
Your Majesty, the representatives of Guangdong Mineral Corporation International are now in the visitors' lobby. They have been searched and are ready to meet you, Sir, as scheduled. Security has already dispossessed them of their passports.

The King nods at the dwarf and continues to play his game of chess. The orderly bows again. Exeunt OLOWOLAGBA. *Shortly, he re-enters ushering* DR FONG CHENG MUK, *an executive Chinese male, and* DR SHIN LIN, *an executive Chinese female. The trio stands attentively in the lounge section of the office; a prelude to introductions.* OLOWOLAGBA *coughs, to draw the King's attention from the chess game. The King looks up and nods. The dwarf bows. Exeunt* OLOWOLAGBA.

DR FONG CHENG MUK
(*Courteously*) Your Majesty, my name is Dr Fong Cheng Muk. (*Bows*) I am the President of Guangdong Mineral

Corporation International. Allow me to introduce Dr Shin Lin, Chairwoman of the Board running the organisation's entire African investments portfolio.

KING LIMA
(*Rises. The representatives bow unanimously and stand erect. He comes round, shakes their hands, and motions them to sit in sofas. All sit*) I am glad you speak English. An Air Force helicopter will take us on a tour of our unclaimed lands tomorrow, which is Friday the thirteenth. I guess the Chinese don't suffer from *Samhainophobia* –the fear of Halloween.

The visitors laugh nervously. Re-enter OLOWOLAGBA *bearing tea and sliced cakes on veiled trays. He places them on a central coffee table and begins setting cups.*

We have gold, diamonds, asbestos, plutonium and platinum deposits. Our minerals are of the best quality according to the assay reports of many European firms. We'll build cities more mesmerising than London and Sydney. (*Rises and crosses to his desk, picks a trimmed stick and goes to a large relief map on the wall*)

Exeunt OLOWOLAGBA.

(*Indicating*) This whole place has plutonium and coal, not to mention methane gas. (*Lowers the stick and grins*) What is my reward, Dr Fong?

The visitors are dumbfounded.

If you thought you would exploit stupid Africans and their minerals at no extra cost you were dead wrong.

DR FONG CHENG MUK
(*Demurs, speechless. Diplomatically*) Lion of Ngoloi, we are open to further discussions on how we could thank you as a corporation. I'll need to sit down with my board.

KING LIMA
As we speak, sizeable amounts of cocaine have been placed in your hotel rooms. You, the Chinese, execute with the sword. In the US that would be deemed cruel and unusual punishment. We throw drug traffickers at crocodiles. Our punishment is primitive but very effective.

DR SHIN LIN
Sir, we would be happy to learn your acceptable tribute, if I may use that word.

KING LIMA
Ten million US dollars upfront plus ten per cent of your annual profits. You'll put the ten per cent profit share on an affidavit in both English and Mandarin. I shall appear on your corporate papers as a shareholder in all your local ventures. By end of day tomorrow, the ten million shall have been transferred into a Swiss bank account whose number I'll give you. If you are in agreement, rise and bow now. If you disagree, remain seated. The police will fetch you in a moment —already I have your passports. You cannot leave this kingdom.

The delegates exchange baffled glances, demur, then rise and bow, their faces deadpan.

Dr Fong and Dr Shin Lin, enjoy the delicacies before you. My lawyers and Mandarin translators will join us shortly to help us document our agreement.

The King smiles and crosses towards them, his hand outstretched for a handshake.

Curtain

Scene Two

Same night
The legislator's master bedroom

[Act 2]

HON. KATOMENE, *alone, shirtless and barely covered in a pyjamas trousers, is lying in bed, snoring drunkenly. A telephone handset, an open Bible, rosary beads, a wristwatch, an almost empty bottle of vodka and a glass are on a bedside table near his head. His wife's position is vacant but indicative of earlier occupation. The telephone rings. He jerks awake, snaps on a shaded bedside lamb and snatches the receiver as he props up on an elbow.*

KATOMENE

(*Groggy and drunken*) Hello, sergeant! Hello! (*Listens*) O! I am sorry, Bishop. I thought the police were calling us. (*Listens and crosses himself clumsily*) And also with you. (*Listens as he reaches for his rosary beads and wears them around his neck*) It is right to give Him thanks and praise. (*Listens*) Not yet, Bishop Hasbrouck; she hasn't been found. No one called us or the police. I believe whoever did it will call – (*Listens after being interrupted*) No. I always make that satanic mistake, Your Lordship.(*Listens*) Yes, I believe in the Holy Spirit, the holy Catholic Church, the communion of saints, the forgiveness of sins, the resurrection of the body, and the life everlasting. (*Listening, he crosses himself again and sits on the edge of the bed, his feet on a rag*) Yes, we can pray together, Your Lordship. (*Kneels quickly and prays aloud over the receiver*) **Our Father in heaven, holy be Your Name, Your kingdom come, your will be done on earth as in heaven. Give us today our daily**

119

bread. Forgive us our sins as we forgive those who sin against us. Do not bring us to the test but deliver us from evil. (*Listens still kneeling*) Amen. (*Listens*) And also with you. (*Listens as he resumes his sit on the bed's edge*) My wife is reasonably coping, Bishop, but often she breaks down sobbing. The McLeods are also running around. Their son has been to the city morgue and mortuary among other places. (*Listens*) Yes, Your Lordship. And also with you. Thank you for calling, Your Lordship. Good night, Bishop Hasbrouck.

He cradles the receiver, shakes his head stoically for a while, and then grabs the bottle of vodka, gulps twice and belches loudly, wincing, and sets the bottle on the table. Without looking, he gropes in vain behind him for his wife, and turns sharply to stare at a vacant position in the bed.

Where's this woman? (*Looks about, seated*) Belemina! Belemina! Are you in the loo? Hurry up, the bishop called! The man of God is praying for Mimudeh as I speak! We need to join him in prayer now that it's about midnight! (*Pauses*) Woman, where the heck are you? (*Shakes his head, checks the time on the wristwatch on the table, shakes his head again and wears the watch*) It's a quarter to midnight. Soon it's going to be Friday the thirteenth. I am not in the mood for Halloween jokes!

He rises and crosses to a closet, from which he draws a dressing gown, dons it and vanishes briefly into the en suite bathroom.

KATOMENE'S VOICE (OFF-STAGE)
Where the heck is she? *Paraskevidekatriaphobia* is movie stuff. Jesus! She left the water running... nearly flooded

the house! This woman is demonic! We are in dire need of an exorcist in this diocese! Now Mimudeh's disappearance is fuelling her demons! (*Sound of a flashing cistern follows*) I believe the Virgin Mother struggles to keep Belemina sane! I believe I entered into a wrong marriage! The **sangoma** made it clear she was worse than a whore! I believe I must start life afresh – (*Voice stops abruptly*) No, I don't believe in starting life anew! I believe in the Holy Spirit, the holy Catholic Church, the communion of saints, the forgiveness of sins, the resurrection of the body, and the life everlasting!

He emerges from the bathroom wiping his hands on the gown and, swearing inaudibly, exits into a dark passage leaving the bedroom door open. The passage is soon lit. The noise of doors opening and banging follows. Re-enter the legislator hurriedly, worried.

KATOMENE

No sign of her. Her car isn't in the garage. It's midnight. What the heck is going on?

He switches on the bedroom's main lights, crosses drunkenly to the headboard, takes his cell-phone and pistol from a drawer and makes a call, pacing impatiently, nervously.

(*Holding the cell-phone against his ear*) Answer the call! Answer! Answer, Belemina! (*Listens then abruptly*) Belemina, where're you? (*Listens*) Who am I talking to? (*Listens*) Sergeant Gopo? No. I need to speak to my wife. This is my wife's number, damn it! (*Listens*) You were about to call me? What is going on, please? Just handover the cell-phone to its owner! I am the husband –Katomene Hasa! (*Listens for a while, sinks on the edge of the bed and continues to listen. Calmly*) Let me see if I follow. You said you are Sergeant Gopo. You found my wife's cell-phone in a handbag she left on a security counter on the ground floor of Fitzroy House. (*Listens*) Unbelievable! (*Listens*) My wife is on the roof and threatening to jump? (*Rises gingerly*) I know where it is! I am on my way, Sir!

Now trembling, he puts his cell-phone on the headboard, slides the pistol behind his back into the waistband of his pyjamas, draws a pair of slippers under the bed, wears them and dashes to the exit. Exeunt KATOMENE.

Curtain

Scene Three

**Same night
In front a tall building
(Fitzroy House) in the CBD**

[Act 2]

A uniformed policeman promptly takes drunken KATOMENE, *in the same clothes as the previous scene, to a police sergeant,* SGT GOPO, *who is looking up the building amid four unsettled firemen. Ambulance and police lights are sweeping the scene and the façade. The sergeant is holding a megaphone. In the periphery, a policeman is maintaining a wide berth between the scene and a curious, off-stage crowd. The policeman who ushered the legislator crosses to the other side to help with mob control.*

KATOMENE
I am Hon. Katomene Hasa. What is going on, Sergeant?

SGT GOPO
We have a situation, Honourable. (*Pointing skywards*) Your wife is on the roof.

KATOMENE
(*Looking up*) There is no one up there. I don't see anyone. (*Glances at his wristwatch*) Friday the thirteenth has just begun. If this is some joke I'll sue the police –mark my words.

SGT GOPO

She left her car keys, a handbag and a suicide note in the foyer. A security guard we presume had fallen asleep later saw the note and called the police.

KATOMENE

If it's Belemina up there I must talk to her.

SGT GOPO

You can't. She bolted the door to the roof. No one can reach her. (*Looking up and speaking into the megaphone*) MRS HASA, YOUR HUSBAND IS HERE! HE BEGS YOU TO COME DOWN! NO CHARGES WILL BE LAID AGAINST YOU! JUST COME DOWN AND WE ALL GO HOME! (*To the legislator*) This is where the problem is; she is not communicating at all.

KATOMENE

(*Stretching a hand for the megaphone*) Let me talk to her, Serge.

SGT GOPO

A police psychologist is on his way. He's the only one who can authorise you to talk to her under the circumstances.

KATOMENE

(*Enraged*) Damn it! She's my wife! (*Shows him a ringed finger*) We can't just wait.

SGT GOPO

That is procedure, Honourable. (*Through the megaphone, looking up*) MRS HASA, YOUR HUSBAND IS HERE TO

TAKE YOU HOME! NO CHARGES WILL BE FILED AGAINST YOU!

KATOMENE

(*Looking up*) Are you sure my wife or some lunatic is on that damn roof? I don't see anyone up there! Must be a mistake! Belemina can't be on that roof, I bet my faith. (*Pauses, still looking up*) O! There she is! My God! That is Belemina! What the devil is going on? I don't believe this. (*Improvises a megaphone with his hands*) Belemina! Belemina, please understand! It's me, Katomene! Come down, please! You are creating an unwarranted scene!

SGT GOPO

She can't hear a thing. Fitzroy has eight storeys and there is too much wind up there. (*Through the megaphone*) YOU ARE STANDING ON THE EDGE! PLEASE STEP BACK, MRS HASA! SUICIDE WON'T BRING BACK YOUR DAUGHTER! WE ARE ALL CONCERNED AND HOPING FOR THE BEST!

KATOMENE

(*Skywards*) O! Thank God she has stepped back. But now we can't see her. (*Lowers his gaze*) You said she wrote a note. Where is it?

SGT GOPO

Honourable, the note is now a tagged piece of exhibit in our custody.

KATOMENE

Exhibit against who? What did she write?

SGT GOPO

She gave Mimudeh's kidnappers an hour to call you or any police station. Didn't you listen to the news at eleven? She used her Smartphone to email an ultimatum to the national broadcaster. It was read on both radio and TV. (*Glances at his wristwatch*) The ultimatum expires in two minutes. No fire-engine ladder can reach that height. We have no helicopter, and in any case, it might prompt her to jump.

KATOMENE

(*Desperately*) What are you going to do? Tell me; I am drunk. I can't think straight at the moment. But we are not going to stand here and witness her splatter to her death. I think I must inform our abbot and bishop. The men of God can bring her down.

SGT GOPO

Until we exhaust all our efforts, we'll not entertain outside interventions. The police psychologist promised he would get her down safely. (*Looks up briefly*) Let's hope he gets here before it's too later.

KATOMENE *paces nervously. A booming wail of an ambulance reaches them. It increases to a crescendo and terminates with an addition of flashing lights on the scene and façade. Enter* DR SADA, *the Police Psychologist, in a white dustcoat. The psychologist is leading and directing two paramedics bearing a sheet-covered, "LIMP PATIENT" on an ambulance stretcher. The "patient" is in a neck brace and a face-obscuring oxygen mask and seemingly undergoing a fluid transfusion.*

126

As the paramedics set the stretcher in front of the building,
KATOMENE *and* SGT GOPO *come and stoop over the "patient".*
The psychologist, pointing at the "patient" and the rooftop, talks to the
sergeant briefly, and stands aside, so do the paramedics. Everyone looks
skywards.

SGT GOPO

*(Through the megaphone)*MRS HASA, PLEASE LOOK
DOWN! *(Pauses)* YES, THANK YOU, MADAM!
MIMUDEH HAS BEEN FOUND! THE KIDNAPPERS
HEEDED YOUR PLEA! BUT SHE IS TOO
DEHYDRATED TO SPEAK TO YOU NOW! COME
DOWN AND ACCOMPANY HER TO THE HOSPITAL!
(Pauses) YOU ARE NOW JEOPARDISING YOUR
DAUGHTER'S LIFE! IF YOU ARE COMING DOWN
NOW WAVE AT ME! *(Pauses)* THANK YOU! YOU
BETTER HURRY NOW, MRS HASA!

In relief, everyone lowers their gaze.

(To the legislator and the psychologist) She's on her way down,
gentlemen. If she takes the lift on the eighth floor, she'll be
down here in a minute. If she decides to take the stairs it will
be about four or so minutes.

The two men nod, look at their wristwatches and, like everyone,
stand facing the entrance of the building. In under a minute, enter
BELEMINA *running towards the strapped "patient" on the stretcher.*
She stoops over the "patient", stares down baffled, and begins to retreat
nervously. One of the two peripheral policemen intercepts and handcuffs
her.

Curtain

Act Three

Scene One

Midday
A palatial flower garden-cum-golf course

RADIMIR IVANOV *is setting a two-chair fresco table laden with exquisite silvery dishware, two wineglasses and a bottle of champagne. Enter* JEFFERSON *in a costly tracksuit and a sports cap and towing a golf kit. He draws four balls from the kit, lines them meticulously on a teeing ground away from the table, rises and begins to inspect the clubs, polishing the heads of some with a handkerchief.*

Enter KING LIMA, *in white golf attire, gently stirring a blind-folded, grinning* MIMUDEH *in a sleeveless, red silken mini-dress and stilettos. Her jewellery is exquisite and her hair is expensively groomed. An Elastoplasts bandage is below her larynx, and her palms are still bandaged across. The King leads her to the table, draws a chair for her, sets her down and removes the blindfold from her eyes as the butler pours champagne into the glasses. Breathless, the girl marvels at the lavish dishware, the King standing behind her.*

KING LIMA
(*Going to take his seat facing hers*) Many people, including intellectuals, think that trustworthiness, a great sense of humour and compatibility are the criteria for choosing a partner. (*Grins*) Hunters and gatherers prize beauty and youthfulness in a woman. (*Sits facing her*)

129

The butler unveils the silverware and opens some dishes to reveal scrumptious food on the girl's side of the table, and a bowl of apples and a small, summoning bell near the King. A large, dome-lidded food warmer is in the centre of the table. The butler steps back and bows. Exeunt IVANOV.

Using a fork and a knife, but often her bare hands, MIMUDEH begins to wolf the food and sip the wine, seemingly oblivious to the King's presence. The King picks an apple and munches it staring at her as she eats gluttonously.

Women look for a deep pocket by design. God knew they would need support while raising children. Olo, my orderly, enlightened me recently that God provided Adam with an orchard first so that Eve wouldn't reject him. Nowadays some pastors are telling their congregants the truth —that poverty is a sin, a satanic affliction.

While JEFFERSON busies himself with the clubs, Mimudeh continues to eat, noncommittal. KING LIMA picks the bell, rings it and sets it down. He leaves the table and goes to pull a club from the golf kit. The henchman stands aside. Enter IVANOV after a moment. The butler bows and stands still.

(*Taking setup position for a tee shot, his back to the girl*) What is in the warmer, Mr Radimir Ivanov? Is it Japanese sushi, Bolognese spaghetti or Chinese noodles?

The King aligns himself and begins making pre-swings while MIMUDEH continues to wolf the food. IVANOV crosses to the table and lifts the lid, revealing a large stack of bundled hundred-dollar US banknotes. MIMUDEH *stops munching and, frozen, stares at the money. The butler sets the lid on the table.*

(*His focus still on the ball*) Yester-night I had a meeting with my Chinese business partners. I happened to mention you and my excitement over our pending marriage. They donated ten million dollars as an expression of their happiness. Before you is what they brought in cash this morning. The Chinese are our heartfelt friends. You'll spoil yourself and your parents a little. (*Repositions his feet, his eyes still on the ball*) Radimir Ivanov, ask Prof Pitoni to present himself now. The doctor of philosophy shouldn't be kept waiting. What would we do without intellectuals and technocrats?

The butler bows at the King. Exeunt IVANOV. *The King inhales, flings the club behind his back, holds his breath and is set to swing the club when he hesitates, inspects the club's head and hands the stick to* JEFFERSON.

(*Selecting another club from the kit*) But that won't exhaust the amount. I suggest you go shopping in New York City, Paris or London. If you desire a Peugeot ONYX you may pass through France. But a red Ferrari would complement your gorgeousness.

MIMUDEH *is speechless. Enter* PROF PITONI *holding a handkerchief to his nose, and bows.*

I hate Greek tragedies and everything that ends in sorrow. I am aware this is Friday the thirteenth of September, but I, being no **triskaidekaphobia** sufferer, decree that there shall be a royal wedding. (*Gets into setup positions and aligns himself*

131

again) I've earned the girl's heart, Uncle. Men shall always be hunters and gatherers.

JEFFERSON *slides the first club into the kit and stands aside again.*

PROF PITONI
(*Breathing through the handkerchief over his nose and mouth*) A wedding you said, Your Majesty? But I've just learned that the girl is a twin. Tradition forbids you from touching such. It is taboo and has the power to dethrone.

KING LIMA
(*Making pre-swings, his focus on the ball*) The wedding shall be disconcertingly extravagant. Mimudeh likes Rihanna and Beyoncé. The divas shall perform at the ceremony. (*Pauses*) If indeed she is a twin, you'll give her parents a cow as appeasement. The royal family and hers will perform joint rituals to assuage offended gods and spirits.

PROF PITONI
(*Lowers the handkerchief*) Sovereign, with all due respect, this is a fusion of algebra and alchemy. Not even a draughtsman can square a circle and insert it in a triangle. How are we going to handle her parents and public outcry? (*Covers his nose again with the handkerchief*)

KING LIMA
At sixteen, Mimudeh has reached the age of consent. (*Changes teeing side and begins setup and alignment again*) I abide by the rule of law, Prof Pitoni. (*Points the head in his intended direction of the ball, closing one eye and aiming with the shaft*) Since

you've failed to silence the legislator forever, it's now your duty to convince him to be a father-in-law. (*Determinedly, he lowers the club to the ball and aligns again*) Use all the flowery language you learnt at Oxford. You shall have the honour to present a pride-price to her parents. In the meantime, three gifted women from Kapakasa Village will coach her in sexual prowess.

The King finally attempts the tee shot, PROF PITONI *cringing as the club swings and misses the ball. The King swerves and staggers laughing as he throws the club down and crosses to rejoin the girl at the table. The henchman picks the club, dusts it with his handkerchief, bags it, bows and tows away the kit. Exeunt* JEFFERSON. *The King staring at her once again,* MIMUDEH *resumes wolfing the food and the wine. Suddenly asthmatic,* PROF PITONI *labours to breathe.*

(*Seated; his back to his advisor, his eyes on the girl*) A word of advice, Professor; the blooms are iridescent but the air is lethally-laden with pollen. If I were you I would start moving before I risked hospitalisation. Olowolagba will tell you that your instructions are as clear as God's thoughts over Jeremiah.

The professor rubs his chest with one hand, the other holding the handkerchief over his nose and mouth. His breathing becomes loud and erratic.

(*His eyes still riveted on the girl*) One final thing, Professor; encourage our people to donate cattle for the pending wedding feast. Though we honour the same ideals of truth, gentleness and justice as Englishmen, Scotsmen and

Frenchmen, my people remain Bantu at heart. They understand the essence of tribute.

The professor staggers in a stupor and sinks on his knees. MIMUDEH stops eating and points at the advisor, but the King points at the food, urging her to eat. The professor drops the handkerchief, loosens his necktie and vainly touches his pockets for his inhaler. A severe heart-attack seems to follow. Prof PITONI *clutches his chest and slumps to the ground.*

Curtain

Scene Two

Same afternoon
A private hospital room

[Act 3]

BELEMINA *is lying strait-jacketed and strapped to a bed*, DR DICKSON *and* DR SADA, *the Police Psychologist, are peering into her eyes with a pen-torch and reviewing her records respectively. Enter a policeman ushering* KATOMENE HASA, BISHOP HASBROUCK, *in his purple skullcap*, and FATHER TITO. *The priests are in business suits and crucifixes. The legislator is in a formal shirt and trousers. The policeman closes the door and stands guard.* BELEMINA *is feeding intravenously, and, staring fixedly, is oblivious to no one's presence. The two doctors stand back,* DR SADA *holding the clipboard with the patient's records.*

KATOMENE

(*Holds* BELEMINA's *hand and speaks soothingly*) Belemina, it's me... your husband. Are you alright? Look at me. I've come to take you home. Bishop Hasbrouck and Father Tito are here. Everything will be alright. I've His Lordship's word.

BELEMINA *remains motionless.* KATOMENE *glances at the doctors.*

DR SADA

She refused to eat. Neither was she talking. I am sure you remember me, Hon. Hasa. We met yesterday night at Fitzroy. I am the police psychologist who duped your wife into

135

leaving the roof. This is Dr Dickson, a psychiatrist responsible for her here. He sedated her an hour ago.

KATOMENE
(*Shakes* DR DICKSON's *hand*) It's a pleasure to meet you, Doctor Dickson, though the circumstances are excruciating. This is His Lordship, Bishop Hasbrouck and our abbot, Father Tito. They share our grief.

The priests civilly shake hands with the doctors.

DR DICKSON
I am pleased to meet you, Honourable. It's gratifying to see you are coping.

KATOMENE
I am trying to cope, Doctor. We need to take her home. You think she has lost her mind?

The arrivals briefly gather around BELEMINA, *their faces solemn.*

DR SADA
Your daughter was kidnapped three days ago. There are no indications whether your daughter is alive or dead, within the kingdom or outside. (*Pauses*) Your wife can't face this crisis. She would rather die than wait to hear terrible news.

BISHOP HASBROUCK
Why is she in a strait-jacket?

DR SADA

Attempting suicide is a crime; that is number one. Number two: she is now a potential danger to herself.

BISHOP HASBROUCK

What do we do to get her out?

DR DICKSON

Your Lordship, she must accept the possibility that the worst has happened to their daughter. Assuming the worst is a good starting point. She'll require counselling or institutionalisation.

FATHER TITO

We understand that she wrote a suicide note. What're its contents?

DR SADA

She wrote that she loved her husband, Hon. Hasa, and that she missed their daughter. From the letter we can deduce that the attempted suicide was sacrificial. This is my second visit today. I tried to talk to her this morning. She was withdrawn, which was a bad sign. But she didn't look me in the eyes, which meant she was embarrassed by what she did. Embarrassment under the circumstances is a good sign.

BISHOP HASBROUCK

Dr Sada, I appeal to you to release her as soon as she is herself again. We just want to worry about finding Mimudeh. With his wife under arrest we are stranded between two devils.

DR SADA

I am a police psychologist, Your Lordship, but basically I am a policeman. By attempting to take her life she committed an offence. And it is also my duty to protect her from herself. We'll examine her after the weekend. Pray that she performs well.

DR DICKSON

(*Wryly*) Hospitals have their own psychological side-effects on patients. Has she ever attempted to take her life before?

KATOMENE

She is Catholic. She values life and God dearly, that is my understanding of her.

DR SADA

In layman's terms, your wife is putting herself in your daughter's place, which prompts her to take her own life. But I would hasten to assure you that her life and sanity aren't at grave risk.

KATOMENE

(*Looks at his wife pitiably and ineptly feels for her wrist and neck pulse*) You are a strong woman, dear. You'll pull through. Our daughter will be found. It'll end well; that is God's wish and promise. We prayed with the bishop and the abbot for that end. It is well. It is well. (*Kisses her on the lips, stares at her, straightens and rubs tears from his eyes*)

BISHOP HASBROUCK

(*Crossing himself. Solemnly*) It is well with thee. It is well with thy husband. It is well with the child. (*Kisses the crucifix hanging on his chest and bows his head prayerfully*)

FATHER TITO

As a policeman, Dr Sada, what is your interpretation of Mimudeh's case?

DR SADA

At the moment no clues have presented for anyone to speculate on motive. Apart from the fact that the criminals are dramatic and seem to have a Christian influence, we are finding it difficult to profile them.

FATHER TITO

By the grace of God she will turn out alive. But, Doctor, will she be her same innocent self again?

DR SADA

Father, kidnapping breaks a child. Her perspective at the world and the adults around her will be altered. I must say her future judgements will be founded on mistrust if she fails to go through proper counselling, or God doesn't intervene, so to speak.

BISHOP HASBROUCK

What can we do to ensure Mrs Hasa's release?

DR SADA

Dr Dickson and I will assess her again for signs of mental stability, or lack thereof. And, of course, she must pay an admission of guilt fine. It's a small amount though, but she has the option of appearing before a magistrate if she thinks otherwise. I trust we all believe in the law.

BISHOP HASBROUCK

(*Sternly, his voice sangfroid*) We believe in the Holy Spirit, the holy Catholic Church, the communion of saints, the forgiveness of sins, the resurrection of the body, and the life everlasting.

The bishop, the abbot and the legislator cross themselves in unison.

Curtain

Scene Three

Afternoon
The Prime Minister's office

[Act 3]

PM GAMATO *is consulting some statutes, files and several documents on his desk. Behind him hangs the national flag on a pole. Enter* JEFFERSON *in a dark business suit. The Prime Minister lifts his gaze and stares at him.*

JEFFERSON
(*Walking into the office*) Your Excellency, my name is Jefferson Buckley. I am here to deliver kindly to you a parcel from His Majesty, King Lima III.

PM GAMATO
You should've dropped it on my PA's desk. What happened to our excellent delivery channels?

JEFFERSON
I work under express instructions, Your Excellency. (*Draws a fat envelope from a pocket in his jacket, and places it before the PM*) You'll open it in my presence, sir.

PM GAMATO
(*Staring at the envelope before him*) What is inside... a bomb?

JEFFERSON
Who would harm a man elected by a good majority? Your Excellency, I insist you open the envelope in my presence.

141

Perhaps we'll start the first day of the week and the second half of September by playing a game–Russian roulette, if you like.

PM GAMATO
You are trespassing. Get out of my office.

JEFFERSON
Then you'll be charged with kidnapping, rape and the murder of a schoolgirl.

PM GAMATO
What're you talking about? (*Takes the envelope, inspects it suspiciously, opens it and draws out photographs. Shuffling the pictures, he looks at them in disbelief*) What is this? (*Throws the pictures at Jefferson's chest, scuttling them all over the office*) You had the girl all along? The King knows about this?

JEFFERSON
(*Unruffled*) The pictures show Prime Minister Ete Gamato and Mimudeh, a schoolgirl. She happens to be Hon. Hasa's daughter. The two are nude and in compromising positions. Any police force under the sun would at least charge you with kidnapping, child molestation, an improper relationship with a minor and, of course, rape.

PM GAMATO
I was never anywhere near the schoolgirl! This is a joke in bad taste!

JEFFERSON

(*Sitting in a visitor's chair*) You've a large following. You are like a rich, contemporary prophet, or some popular African rainmaker. Once we unleash them on the Internet you shall be charged. A judge has been tasked to condemn you. You've only up to the eighteenth of this month – forty-eight hours– to toe the line.

PM GAMATO

(*Cornered*) What does King Lima want from me? What is Prof Pitoni's opinion on this?

JEFFERSON

The learned one is under intensive care in hospital. You'll stop criticising your culture. (*Rises and leans on the desk*) And you'll support the King in his bid to marry Mimudeh. In fact, His Majesty intends to appoint you best man for good measure. Good day, Your Excellency.

The henchman turns and walks towards an exit. Exeunt JEFFERSON.

Curtain

Act Four

Scene One

Same afternoon
The Commander-General's office

PM GAMATO *is sitting across a desk watching* GEN. OFUJI *who is going through the photographs of the previous scene. The PM is in the same suit as the last scene, but his tie is rudely loosened and he looks tired. The general is in decorated military fatigues. The commander's cap is on his desk.*

PM GAMATO
General, you studied in British and Canadian military academies. At some point in your career you were seconded to Brussels as an attaché to our embassy. I take it you embraced human rights and their strict observation all the time.

GEN. OFUJI
For a fact I studied abroad and I once served as a military attaché to the Ngoloi Embassy in Belgium, but it appears, Your Excellency, you were photographed abusing a schoolgirl.

PM GAMATO
General, it is the missing schoolgirl.

GEN. OFUJI

Your Excellency, do you mean Hon. Katomene Hasa's daughter?

The Prime Minister nods. The general stares at him.

PM GAMATO

It's not what it seems, General. The photographs were doctored. They were delivered to me less than three hours ago. Someone is trying to blackmail me.

GEN. OFUJI

Tell me about it, Your Excellency. No office is as secure as mine in the whole kingdom.

PM GAMATO

General, you took an oath of allegiance twice this year. Turning against your principal could be interpreted as treasonous. But I know you as an objective man; a fire-fighter in a fire outbreak, a rationalist in times of anarchy and upheavals. When troopers gun-down demonstrators, you court marshal them before a shrewd tribunal. Half a dozen have been executed as a result. I came to you for the sole reason that you are the ultimate lifesaver or hangman.

GEN. OFUJI

Sir, you speak like a seasoned orator whose coming was premeditated. I don't see why the King would kidnap a schoolgirl. He has thousands of willing maidens to choose from. This year over forty thousand girls attended the Reed Dance.

PM GAMATO

General, the King is a sexual gourmand. Every man controlled by his feelings is criminal.

GEN. OFUJI

I am a career soldier. (*Rising*) I earned my rank and decorations. (*Erect and straightening his uniform*) Child abuse is not only illegal but evil. (*Crosses to a set of glassware and a Smirnoff bottle on a tray on a small cabinet in a corner and pours a measure in a glass*) Sir, this is a very tragic moment in our history. The pivotal question is whether or not His Majesty has the audacity to kidnap a schoolgirl. How do you expect a mortal like me to believe your story and claim of innocence?

PM GAMATO

On Wednesday they shall drag me from my office like a rabid dog, arrest and kill me. That is when you shall see the truth of the matter. After I am gone, Mimudeh shall turn up alive or dead, and it shall be charged on me posthumously. (*Pauses*) The Royal Guard and its brigadier are under your command, General. A member or two of the Guard will vouch to seeing Mimudeh at one of the King's numerous residences. Then my blood shall be on your hands.

GEN. OFUJI

In don't believe in God, Your Excellency. I believe in training, strategy, loyalty and a meticulous delivery of duty. If I say the word, guns and cannons will roar, Mig-fighters will criss-cross the territory and it can be Armageddon for everyone in this kingdom. (*Pauses and sips*) But I believe in dreams. It might sound phantasmagorical, but when I was a private thirty-eight years ago, my wife saw me in a dream. She saw me rising above every rank to become the commander-general. This same woman dreamt of you two nights ago. You were stricken and limping towards me for help.

PM GAMATO

This is a Pontius Pilate allusion, General! Your wife is a prophetess of God; therefore you believe in God. Every form of belief is ultimately belief in God.

GEN. OFUJI

I am a man of ethics. (*Demurs*) Many things are offensive in this petticoat-government kingdom. (*Sips and returns to his chair nursing the glass*) What is the way forward then, Your Excellency? Do you have a proposal?

PM GAMATO

We must force the King to abdicate the monarchy. I propose an Instrument of Abdication.

GEN. OFUJI

Why a piece of paper when the Air Force and the Mechanised Brigade are at my disposal? How practicable is your proposal?

PM GAMATO

It's a historical gentlemanly coup. In recent years it happened at the Vatican –the resignation of Pope Benedict XVI. If Rome had wise men during the time of Julius Caesar, this is what they should have done to their great general, and banished him from Roman soil.

GEN. OFUJI

Like I said, I am a man of ethics, Your Excellency; my defence forces won't protect a criminal. But foremost I must interrogate everything. The bottom line is whether Mimudeh is a captive in the King's custody. If indeed she is, the army will rescue her and abolish the monarchy. (*Takes a pen and notepad*) How do we word an Instrument of Abdication, Your Excellency?

PM GAMATO

(*Reaching into an inner pocket in his jacket*) I prepared a draft, General. (*Draws a folded piece of typed paper and unfolds it. Reading*) **I, King Lima III, King of Ngoloi, do hereby declare my irrevocable determination to renounce the throne for myself, my wives and my children, and desire that immediate effect be given this Instrument of Abdication.** (*Places the draft in front of the general*)

GEN. OFUJI

(*Studies the draft pensively and nods*) Your Excellency, you've crafted a nuclear bomb more devastating than any in the history of mankind. This one can completely erase Manhattan.

PM GAMATO

General, you and I will pre-sign this document as witnesses.

GEN. OFUJI

But, Your Excellency, do you think the Anglicized catastrophe will append his signature on this document?

What if he refuses to look at the Instrument, worse still sign it?

PM GAMATO

General, you are a soldier, a man of war. You know when to pull the trigger. Tsar Nicholas' abdication was the worst. They gang-raped his family in his eyes and sodomised him. (*Rises. Sarcastically*) Long live the Lion of Ngoloi.

The general dons his cap, rises, salutes and shakes the Prime Minister's hand firmly across the desk.

Curtain

Scene Two

Morning
An atrium enclosure to a rustic shrine

[Act 4]

Nothing is in sight apart from an open entrance to the shrine, red strips of cloths hang as pendants, animal skulls and effigies. The shrine's entrance is Igloo-like and covered with a red cloth and strings of beads and amulets.

KATOMENE'S VOICE (OFF-STAGE)
Slapping the *sangoma* wasn't a good move after all. We are in a mess now.

BELEMINA'S VOICE (OFF-STAGE)
Shhhh! We are at her shrine now. What do you benefit from regret? Has it ever raised the dead?

KATOMENE *and* BELEMINA, *both hesitant, the former carrying the diviner's bag and goatskin, appear in the enclosure and stare at the open entrance.* KATOMENE *steps forward, but* CHUCHU's *growl from the shrine stops him in his tracks. Both exchange fearful glances and crouch.*

KATOMENE
(*To the shrine. In an attitude of supplication*) We come in peace, *Sangoma*!

CHUCHU'S VOICE (OFF-STAGE)

You pointed a gun at me–a Royal *Sangoma*! (*1st masculine voice*) Your wife slapped me, a Royal *Sangoma*! (*2nd masculine voice*) The dead rule the living. Here we are as many as the storms of the Sahara!

KATOMENE

We apologise sincerely. Name the fine, *Sangoma*!

CHUCHU'S VOICE (OFF-STAGE)

Death! Death and mayhem! (*1st masculine voice*) Death and mayhem to you, your family and every member of your clan! (*2nd masculine voice*) Out of my sight! Out! Out of my sight now!

The couple lower their heads to the ground in humility. A smoking clay pot is tossed out the entrance, shattering on impact in front of them and releasing leaves, charms and bound twigs. Leaving the bag and the goatskin on the ground, the couple rise, startled. BELEMINA clutches her husband's clothes and both retreat.

CHUCHU'S VOICE (OFF-STAGE)

If you won't go away I'll come out and you'll see my wrath!

KATOMENE *and* BELEMINA *exchange fearful glances. Both kick their shoes off.*

KATOMENE

(*Nervously*) State the fine, *Sangoma*!

A baby begins to cry behind the red curtain. The crying rises to a shrill. BELEMINA covers her ears with her hands, but the crying suddenly stops. Stooping, the legislator gingerly tip-toes to the entrance, pulls aside the red curtain and strings, and peers inside.

(*Fearfully, peering inside*) **Sangoma**! Great **Sangoma**! By pointing a gun at you, I wronged the spirits. By slapping you, my wife also erred most grievously. (*Cranes his neck*) Belemina, you won't believe it; there is no one inside. I can see only a log fire and spiritual paraphernalia, mostly gourds. There are three clay busts arranged in a line. The busts are sitting on small rock pedestals. Human hair and chicken feathers are stuck in their scalps. (*Turns and looks at her*) It must be the ones which were talking all along.

BELEMINA *motions that he makes a submission.* KATOMENE *takes out a wad of banknotes from a hip pocket, turns and shows it to Belemina, who nods, and tosses it into the shrine.* CHUCHU *quietly appears behind them barefoot in a trance and in divination regalia. A bead pocket is tied around her waist.*

CHUCHU
(*Startling them into cringing*) Hey! You tossed US $500, €50 and a few dollars of our worthless money. That was the fine for the violence you perpetrated against her. For seeing her underwear, you shall pay with similar amounts.

BELEMINA *retreats to* KATOMENE *and the two kneel facing her in humility by the entrance, their cheeks on the ground.*

Because she walked ungirded from your house while possessed by a masculine spirit, you shall bring a black bull for appeasement rituals, or I foresee your wife running amok naked before committing suicide. (*Growls*) Thank the spirits; I foresee you fulfilling my demand within the week. (*Abruptly*) By coming to your house ten days ago she offended the Lion of Ngoloi. He is now our common enemy.

KATOMENE

(*Looks up still crouched*) We are sorry to hear that, *Sangoma*.

CHUCHU

(*Prancing*) By humiliating the spirits you brought misfortune into your house. Where is your daughter? Is it not a week now since she was snatched?

BELEMINA

(*Her cheek on the ground*) If her disappearance is due to a curse you placed on us, we beseech you to lift it.

CHUCHU

(*In a rage*) Quick to strike like lightening that kills what it won't eat, woman, talk to me through your husband!

KATOMENE

Where is she, *Sangoma*? Is she alive?

CHUCHU

Your posture offends the spirits behind you. Sit down and cross your legs.

The couple complies. The diviner draws bones from the pocket of beads around her waistline and casts them on the ground.

154

(*Reading the bones strewn on a wide area*) I see two spears in a blacksmith's furnaces. A voice tells me they are yours. But I see your enemy's hands poking the embers. I also see your Mimudeh...a bundle of fear on a bed of roses. As the north wind seduces the south wind in endless whirlwinds, I see her more closely. I see a magnificent house in which dust is not allowed to settle. A vulture circles over her, descending slowly like the wrath of the spirits. (*Growls*) I hear drumbeat. I see her lying naked on a reed mat. I see sharp white thorns and her almond, black pumpkins. Her face is covered. Her vineyard is bare, but I see a footprint on it. O! The thorns want to pierce her gyrating pumpkins. She sways and wriggles. I hear the applause of three elderly women.

BELEMINA
Sangoma, who took her captive and what do they want?

CHUCHU
Woman, this is your second and final warning! Talk to me through your husband. (*to Katomene*) Were you blind when you married this undesirable, noisy owl?

A tense silence follows.

KATOMENE
Sangoma, who took her captive and what do they want?

CHUCHU
(*Crosses to an animal skull mounted on the periphery, caresses its temples and appeals to it*) Spirit of prophecy and hindsight, who took her captive and what do they want? You skull, whose soul is in the sky watching everything, shed light. You

ancestors in the land of the dead and the unborn, to whom nothing is hidden, give me a portrait. You cave-dwelling gods ever cradled on Tuesday, give me a name.

Her eyes on the skull, CHUCHU *is astounded and retreats.*

KATOMENE
What are the bones saying, Great *Sangoma*?

CHUCHU
(*Her eyes riveted on the skull*) An iron hand in a velvet glove took her. In public, he is gentle, like the caressing feel of silk. In private, he is a ferocious inferno.

KATOMENE
Who is this man, *Sangoma*?

CHUCHU
(*Picking the bones she cast*) The African rock python is a very deceptive snake. It captivates its would-be victim with its colours and gracious movements. (*Savagely, jerking her hands*) Then it pounces, coils around the victim and breaks all their ribs! (*Looks at the skull again and trembles, dropping the bones*) I see a demigod... a mortal, a contemporary man. He rides on ancestral winds prevailing far into the future. With one hand he can render death and, with the other, nurse a baby, both at the same time. Though he is reptilian and predatory, he charms teenage girls. He has placed a rose in your daughter's hand.

KATOMENE

(*Pleading*) Give us a name and an address, Great *Sangoma*.

CHUCHU *stares at him and begins to growl.*

Curtain

Scene Three

Midday

The Commander-General's office

[Act 4]

GEN. OFUJI *is standing at the file cabinet in the corner fixing himself a tot of Smirnoff while* LT. GEN. DRAGO, *browsing through a printed sheaf of papers bearing the Government's insignia, is sitting in a visitor's chair at his desk. Both men are in combat fatigues; the lieutenant-general is wearing his rank cap while the Commander General's is on his desk beside a portable radio that is sounding a news jingle drumbeat before it launches into a news bulletin.*

FEMININE VOICE (RADIO)

Good afternoon, Ngoloi, welcome to the Wednesday midday news on your favourite station. In a disturbing twist to Mimudeh's disappearance, her parents, Hon. Katomene Hasa and his wife, alleged this morning that women working on express orders from His Majesty, King Lima III, kidnapped their daughter on the tenth of September this year. A senior police spokesman, Assistant Commissioner Loebbe Koro, when asked to comment by a correspondent of this paper shortly after the Hasas gave a press conference in the city, stated that the police didn't act on hearsay. Mimudeh's parents said they were going to file an urgent application in the High Court this morning in an attempt to rescue their daughter from the King's custody. The parents could not be drawn to disclose how they came to allege that the King kidnapped their daughter and that Mimudeh was

159

being held by **King Lima III.** However, a constitutional law advocate practising in the city who requested anonymity, has said that the application was bound to be thrown away with costs since it is criminal and unconstitutional to charge, sue or prefer any litigation against **King Lima III.** In other news –

LT. GEN. DRAGO *turns the radio off.* GEN. OFUJI *sips his tot and bears the glass to his chair.*

GEN. OFUJI
(*Sitting*) How the Hasas have come to that conclusion, we are yet to establish, but it is of no significance to us now. Since a sergeant in the Royal Guard has confirmed seeing a girl matching Mimudeh's description dining with the King at the Regal Golf Course at the main palace, we must move in swiftly. My heart tells me the girl is in the palace. My wife told me the same this morning. The Prime Minister, who was in this office two days ago, was convinced the King kidnapped the schoolgirl. Lt. Drago, our swords are half drawn.

LT. GEN. DRAGO
Yes, General. (*Referring to the sheaf of papers in his hand*) The Instrument provides a peaceful means for his exit. Sir, I await further instruction.

GEN. OFUJI
We'll only furnish him with the Instrument on condition the girl is a captive. I'll step forward and hand him the document. You'll be a few paces away and you'll keep your hand near your pistol. Carry a Jericho 941; it rarely misfires.

But you'll keep a dagger at hand. Brief me on the deployment, Lieutenant General.

LT. GEN. DRAGO

Sir, the Mechanised Brigade is already on its way to the Royal Guard's headquarters, the national broadcaster and the other positions. The gist of the deployment has not been disclosed to the soldiers, Sir.

GEN. OFUJI

Until further notice, no armed soldier or armoured vehicle leaves their barracks without your express permission. Only the Mechanised brigadier and his men enjoy the freedom of the city until further notice. (*Gulps the remnant of the Smirnoff*) I shall try to persuade the Lion to sign, but when I remove my cap that is the signal to shoot.

LT. GEN. DRAGO

Yes, General —three bullets to the chest. When he is down I'll fire three more shots into his cranium like you ordered, Sir.

GEN. OFUJI

(*Nods and wears his cap*) Do you've any questions, Lt. Drago?

LT. GEN. DRAGO

No questions, Sir.

GEN. OFUJI

Blissful! (*Rising*) Execution of the Instrument awaits, Lieutenant.

LT. GEN. DRAGO *places the sheaf of papers on the desk and stands at attention.*

You may want to know what is in it for you, Lieutenant-General.

LT. GEN. DRAGO
Sir, I am motivated by duty. General, I am bound by my loyalty to you.

GEN. OFUJI
That is very noble, Lieutenant, but today –this Wednesday the eighteenth of September – we are making history. This is our bit for the poor souls selling vegetables by the roadside, for our daughters prostituting themselves lame for a pittance. After this deed both of us shall resign and sit pretty for the rest of our lives. The Prime Minister promised that his regime will honour us significantly. I gave His Excellency my word that the army will not take over power. Ngoloi shall forever avoid the military scars of Nigeria. *(Brings his hand up in salute)*

The lieutenant-general brings his up, too, and stands frozen.

Lt. Gen. Drago, I appreciate your valour and subordination to authority. We are departing for the main palace in one hour. Lieutenant, this meeting has come to an end.

LT. GEN. DRAGO
Sir, yes, Sir!

The generals lower their hands in unison. GEN. OFUJI *remains standing while the lieutenant turns and marches towards the exit.* Exeunt LT. GEN. DRAGO.

Curtain

Act Five

Afternoon of same day
The palace's main lounge

MIMUDEH, *in a mini-skirt and hugging top, is sitting across* KING LIMA's *lap, a banquet of red roses in her bandaged hands. An Elastoplasts bandage is still on her larynx. The King, who is in cargo shorts and a T-shirt, is fondling her shoulders as he dozes in a reclining chair. The King finally falls asleep. The girl carefully disentangles herself from him, puts the flowers down, looks about frantically, and quickly tip-toes towards the exit. Exeunt* MIMUDEH, *but shortly enters moving stealthily with a raised sword. She edges towards the King, but is interrupted by approaching whistling when she is set to behead him. She lowers the sword, stows it behind a sofa and rushes to kneel beside him, placing her head on his lap.*

Enter OLOWOLAGBA *whistling, and coughs to wake the King. The monarch wakes and fondles the girl's head. The dwarf bows, steps forward, whispers in the monarch's ear and stands erect. The King dismissively motions the girl in the direction of the exit. She picks the banquet of roses, rises and walks towards the exit. Exeunt* MIMUDEH. *The King rises, a deathly frown on his face. Enter* RADIMIR IVANOV, *bowing and ushering* PM GAMATO *who is bearing an A4 envelope. Exeunt* IVANOV.

PM GAMATO
(Bows) Good morning, Your Majesty. *(Stretches the envelope to the King)*

KING LIMA

State your business, Prime Minister. If you haven't heard, Prof Pitoni– my beloved uncle– succumbed to asthma yesterday. He was comatose for four days. We are in deep shock. You'll have to come back; we have not yet opened a book of condolences.

PM GAMATO

I am afraid I hadn't heard the terrible news, Sir. You've my condolences, Sovereign. But I received a Court Order and a petition this morning from Hon. Hasa and his wife.

KING LIMA

The Hasas... I heard their malicious allegations on the news. But what has the Prime Minister got to do with all of this? (*Arrogantly*) Read the documents. (*Sits angrily*)

The Prime Minister draws two attached printed documents from the envelope. OLOWOLAGBA *remains rooted, listening.*

PM GAMATO

I'll start with the Court Order, Sir. (*Reading*) **In the case of Hon. Katomene Hasa and Mrs Belemina Hasa versus King Lima III filed urgently and heard in my chambers on short notice this day the eighteenth of September, a case in which the monarch had no legal representation, I, Justice Ishmael Mila, ruled in favour of a strong speculation put forward by the plaintiffs that Mimudeh Hasa was kidnapped by two women working for King Lima III.**

I deem the suspected abduction of the schoolgirl illegal and barbaric in the broadest sense, and order that King Lima III surrenders Mimudeh to her parents with immediate effect, failure of which all palatial villas and lodges in the kingdom shall be thoroughly searched by members of the Parliamentary Portfolio Committee on Human Rights assisted by the police.*(Looks at the King)* Sir, Justice Ishmael Mila, a judge of good standing, handed this judgement.

KING LIMA
You read like a veteran BBC newsreader. What is the other document?

PM GAMATO
(Bringing the second sheet to the fore) The petition, Sovereign.

KING LIMA
Read it, Your Excellency.

PM GAMATO
(Reading) **In the name of justice, I, Hon. Katomene Hasa, hereby petition you, Prime Minister Ete Gamato to see to it that King Lima III complies with a High Court Order issued by Justice Ishmael Mila. The monarch must surrender my daughter Mimudeh Hasa as directed. No harm should come to me, my family and Mimudeh as a result. Should you sit on this petition then it shall be clear that the Prime Minister has a complete disregard of the rule of law and is working in cahoots with the King.**

KING LIMA

Justice Mila is a gifted clown. Order the Riot Police to teargas him out of his chambers.

PM GAMATO

But, Your Majesty, is the schoolgirl in your custody by any chance?

KING LIMA

She is my guest. (*Rises*) Do you have qualms with that, Prime Minister?

Enter IVANOV *and bows.*

IVANOV

Your Majesty, the Hasas, Justice Ishmael Mila and the Royal *Sangoma* seek your audience. A boy in school uniform, an advocate, a judge and two priests are accompanying them. All have been searched thoroughly and are in the visitor's lobby. A score of foreign and local journalists are outside the main gate. The major has already issued a final order to the reporters to stand back. Sir, the guards have cocked their rifles.

KING LIMA

Modern journalists are daredevils; hence they perish on foreign battlefronts. It's called civilisation, Radimir Ivanov. (*Resuming his seat*) However, I doubt if the situation is worrisome; Major Vorovo would've notified me.

KING LIMA *sits still, pensive. The butler and the orderly await instructions. Enter* QUEEN MOTHER JIRIMITA *in a headscarf and a matching floor-sweeping African dress.*

QUEEN MOTHER JIRIMITA

(*Entering*) O! This is now akin to drama in Athenian amphitheatres. By bringing with them interrogative Epicureans and Stoics in an attempt to down-dress the Lion, the Hasas bring Areopagus into this palace! The Lion will entertain them as proof that he isn't a coward. His Excellency shall play arbiter. The electorate put him in his office because he believes in a world of facts, justice and fairness, although belief and practicality are always planets apart. (*To the butler and the orderly*) Arrange the furniture suitably and show the babblers in. His Majesty shall quickly dress for the occasion. Queen Jolina and I shall back him. (*Going away*) No policemen or soldiers inside; the Athenians might cry intimidation. (*Exeunt the* QUEEN MOTHER)

The King demurs for a while then rises and follows his mother. Exeunt KING LIMA. *As the Prime Minister idles worrisomely, rolling and unrolling the documents, the orderly and the butler arrange sofas and chairs in segment formation —facing a grandiose chair flanked by two ornamental armchairs. The orderly discovers the stowed sword and keeps it. The butler places a chair near the central threesome and motions the PM to sit on it. The PM sits. Exeunt* IVANOV *and* OLOWOLAGBA, *the latter with the sword.*

Shortly, re-enter RADIMIR IVANOV *ushering* ADV. MBANI, *followed by* JUSTICE MILA, KATOMENE, BELEMINA, ARCHER, BISHOP HASBROUCK and FATHER TITO, *and barefoot* CHUCHU *in beads and a black cloth. The men are in business suits and official regalia, while the priests wear crucifixes. They are courteously motioned to the sofas and chairs arranged in a segment. All sit solemnly.*

Re-enter KING LIMA *in a suit with a tanned leopard sash across the jacket and a matching, leopard toque. He is followed by* QUEEN MOTHER JIRIMITA *and an ethereally-dressed* QUEEN JOLINA. *The King sits in the armchair flanked by his mother to the right, and by* QUEEN JOLINA *to his left. The butler bows at the threesome and crosses to the exit. Exeunt* IVANOV. *A tense moment prevails. The King nods at the Prime Minister who rises nervously, dropping the documents.*

PM GAMATO
Men and women of Ngoloi, I greet you. I am no respecter of petitions and I don't stand here as a Prime Minister, but purely as a responsible citizen who respects meaningful dialogue.

CHUCHU
You speak very well, Prime Minister, but the Lion is baying for my blood.

QUEEN MOTHER JIRIMITA
What makes you say so, *Sangoma*?

CHUCHU
My spirits and my divination bones. They have never lied. The King is my witness.

QUEEN MOTHER JIRIMITA

Where is the evidence, *Sangoma*? Let the matter rest, *Sangoma*, unless you are prepared to face a million-dollar defamation lawsuit.

Re-enter the butler and the orderly bearing large trays laden with delicacies and filled champagne glasses. They move across the visitors offering them the refreshments but nothing is picked. IVANOV *and* OLOWOLAGBA *leave the trays on low tables, bow and exeunt.* ADV. MBANI *rises, approaches the King in profound humility and holds out a rolled and sealed Court Order to* KING LIMA. *The King takes the document, tears it to pieces and drops them dramatically. The advocate bows solemnly as before and returns to his seat.*

PM GAMATO

Turning to you, Hon. Hasa and Mrs Hasa, what can the King do for you now that you've his attention?

KATOMENE

Our daughter is being held here against her will. We are here to salvage her if ever there is anything left of her.

KING LIMA

I, a respecter of human rights, which are also children's rights, a man who has commissioned many child-oriented organisations in this kingdom, am not capable of holding a child captive.

BELEMINA

(*In a rage and pointing*) You trample human rights! You regard other people's daughters as sexual artefacts!

The King stares at her; his countenance deadpan.

PM GAMATO

I'll ask you to withdraw your words, Mrs Hasa. You cannot subject His Majesty to such insult.

BELEMINA

(*Rises in anger*) I stand by my words! This man has no honour! He is a criminal!

QUEEN MOTHER JIRIMITA

Won't you control your wife, Honourable?

KATOMENE

(*Rises*) Self-expression is a universal right, Queen Mother.

PM GAMATO

I pray both of you be seated. Emotions can only derail this meeting.

The Hasas shake their heads in dismay, and resume their seats.

CHUCHU

(*Trance-like*) I see two spears in furnaces!

PM GAMATO

(*Baffled*) Let us not lose focus, ***Sangoma***. The schoolgirl is the pertinent issue.

CHUCHU

(*Rises and sniffs the air, her nose lurching*) I sniff the scent of a twin. I smell virginal blood. Mimudeh is in this palace. If my perceptions are wrong, I denounce my ancestors this instant, and I must expire before sunset. Which I won't do; the girl *is* in this palace. (*Grabbing her cloth*) I'll rent this cloth for the Lion to see my nakedness, and this dynasty shall crumble before the end of the year.

QUEEN MOTHER JIRIMITA
Rent the cloth now, *Sangoma*, or sit down for order's sake! If we wanted circuses we would've flown to Beijing or Moscow.

The diviner growls and resumes her seat.

PM GAMATO
I am no royal apologist, but I think the dispute is whether Mimudeh is a captive in this palace or she is a guest of His Majesty. There is an honourable judge and His Lordship, Bishop Hasbrouck in our midst. I propose that Mimudeh be brought in here. She must choose between her parents and the King. If she chooses the King, we'll all know this was much ado over nothing.

The visitors consult each other mutely, nodding.

Your Majesty, do you object?

KING LIMA
Why would I? I am a man of equity. I've never infringed on anyone's freedom.

PM GAMATO

I propose that Miss Mimudeh Hasa be summoned into this lounge. Thank you. (*Sits*)

Enter OLOWOLAGBA *and bows.*

OLOWOLAGBA

(*Panicky*) Sir, Gen. Ofuji and Lt. Gen. Drago seek your urgent audience. They have just arrived in haste, accompanied by two truckloads of armed troopers. The soldiers are replacing the Royal Guard as I speak. I told the generals that you were in an important meeting. The Commander-General said it could not wait.

KING LIMA

(*Laughs*) My Olowolagba, the General is a professional soldier under oath. He heard the malevolent news and is here to protect the Lion with his life. Intelligence informed me a while ago that the Mechanised Brigade was taking strategic positions in and around the city.

QUEEN MOTHER JIRIMITA

Gen. Ofuji comes at an opportune moment. He'll witness on behalf of the army and himself that His Majesty is a man of equity —that he is a judicious man blessed with a charmer's aura. You'll show the General in, Olowolagba.

The visitors nod approval. KING LIMA *nods at the orderly. The dwarf bows. Exeunt* OLOWOLAGBA. *The King whispers to* QUEEN JOLINA. *The queen nods, rises and saunters out of the lounge.*

QUEEN MOTHER JIRIMITA

(*Sardonically*)It beats me there are subjects in our kingdom who don't believe people fall in love. I am amazed by educated people who want to be taught that love is beyond caste. Every man and woman has a lover of their dreams somewhere in this world. At the right time people fall in love. God help us. (*Looking at Archer*) Mimudeh told me about one Archer McLeod. If you are the one, should other people, for any reason, stand between genuine lovebirds?

ARCHER *stares at the King.* KING LIMA *motions the boy to stand up.* ARCHER *rises.*

ARCHER

Queen Mother, I am a student; therefore I am not well versed in romantic matters. However, I am not amazed there are dreamers in this world who sit in the emptiness of their vain hopes. Christ healed every sickness and infirmity, but He did nothing about the foolishness of fools.

KING LIMA *claps his hands dramatically.*

QUEEN MOTHER JIRIMITA

(*Smiling*) You are a gifted orator who needs limitless support. The Royal Family offers you an open bursary to study at Cambridge or Oxford University. Perhaps you prefer a prestigious one, Harvard for instance?

ARCHER

I am afraid, Your Highness, I cannot accept your scholarship. Let my girlfriend go. (*Resumes his seat*)

175

Re-enter OLOWOLAGBA *ushering* GEN. OFUJI *and* LT. GEN. DRAGO *in combat fatigues and wearing holstered pistols and bayonets. The commander-general is holding a leather dossier. As the orderly bows, the generals click their boots and salute. The three stand aside against a wall. Re-enter* QUEEN JOLINA *leading* MIMUDEH *into the lounge. The schoolgirl is magnificent in a long evening gown. The Elastoplasts bandage is still across her neck and her hands are still bandaged. The girl yells with joy and runs to her parents who rise and embrace her tearfully.* QUEEN JOLINA *resumes her seat to the left of the King.* ARCHER *rises and watches the embracing threesome.* BELEMINA *hurriedly inspects* MIMUDEH, *tears streaming down the mother's cheeks as she looks at her daughter's neck and bandaged hands.* ARCHER *and* MIMUDEH *stare at each other, their faces solemn.*

PM GAMATO

That is enough. (*Rises*) Could Mimudeh stand in the centre, please?

MIMUDEH *slowly retreats to the centre of the lounge while her parents resume their seats, never taking their eyes off their daughter.*

Mimudeh Hasa, if you were kidnapped, I ask that you go to your parents. If you are living freely in this palace and would like to continue to, I ask that you go to His Majesty. (*Pauses*) Now feel free to go where you would please.

A confidence-exuding KING LIMA *rises, so do* BELEMINA *and* KATOMENE. *For a while* MIMUDEH *stands forlornly, fingering the Elastoplasts across her larynx. She looks at her bandaged hands. Gingerly, she turns in the direction of her parents. The parents stretch their arms at their daughter, but she stops, retreats, turns and*

176

crosses to the King. KING LIMA *holds her hands. The girl and the king gaze into each other's eyes, embrace and kiss passionately. All the visitors, except the generals, are shocked, some look away in disgust.* QUEEN JOLINA *rises and claps her hands self-consciously, smiling.* ARCHER *holds his chest, inhales loudly and collapses.*

Curtain

Act Six

Four Years Later....

Epilogue

Evening
A comfy campus hostel room
(University of Cambridge)

ARCHER McLEOD, *in warm clothes and woollen gloves, is sitting at a book-clustered desk browsing the Internet on a laptop, jotting notes and sketching diagrams on a pad. Cell-phone headphones plugged in his ears; he is nodding mildly, rhythmically, occasionally sipping a hot mug of coffee. A knock comes on a door behind him, but he doesn't hear it. It comes again, louder this time. He continues to study. The knock comes for the third time, louder than before. He turns, removing the headphones.*

ARCHER
(*To the door*) It's not locked! Hop in! But I told you I would be reading!

A moment lapses and he reverts to his studies. The knock comes again. ARCHER *sighs aloud, annoyed, and shrugs.*

(*Focused on his studies*) I know it's you, Llewellyn! It's either you want to tell me a naughty Irish joke or you are standing there naked! I wish I was also taking Sociology! Medicine is backbreaking! Now hop in, moron, or vamoose!

The knock comes for the fourth time.

(*Looks at the door*) Hey! You are snapping my nerves, screwball! If you want to continue to be my buddy you must understand, Llewellyn!

He continues to stare at the door. Another moment passes and the knock comes for the fifth time. ARCHER rises, angrily crosses to the door, pulls it open and retreats in shocked disbelief. Enter YEMUDEH in red warm garments and high heels. A visitor's badge is pinned to her clothing. She is carrying a small traveller's bag. ARCHER halts in the centre of the room, and she does the same two paces from him.

(*Stutters*) Mi-Mimudeh! It's been four years now! September the eighteenth once again! And – and you are here! What's happening?

YEMUDEH
I landed and checked into a hotel less than an hour ago. Couldn't get a direct flight and had to fly via Tel Aviv. I was airborne for over twenty-three hours. (*Looks about and smiles*) Archer, or should I say Dr McLeod, aren't you going to offer a lady a seat?

ARCHER
O! Of course, Mimudeh, I am sorry. What's happening to my manners? (*Motioning to a couch beside his desk*) I think I am slipping into something worse than traumatic shock. Please, sit down.

YEMUDEH *crosses to the couch, sets the bag on her lap and sits. He follows her gingerly, sinks on his knees at her feet and looks inquisitively into her eyes.*

(*Voice trailing off emotionally*) Four years, Mimudeh... (*Sticks out four fingers to her*) Four... four solid years! What is a married lady doing in a bachelor's room?

YEMUDEH
(*Clamps his cheeks between her palms*) No, Archer, it's me. Look at me closely. (*Pauses*) It's Yemudeh –her twin.

ARCHER
Christ! It's terrible! You two have always looked like terracotta replicas. O, Yemudeh! Tell me about Mimudeh. How is she? (*Begins to cry, his shoulders lurching, and buries his face on the bag on her lap*)

YEMUDEH
(*Patting and stroking him*) Shhhh. Don't cry, Archer. Crying is sissy. Queen Mimudeh shares your grief. Look at the bright side. The monarch offered you an open bursary though you had arrogantly turned it down. You'll walk out of Cambridge University a specialist doctor. Queen Mimudeh is alive and well, discounting the heartbreak. Life must go on; the way it went on after the Holocaust. (*Pauses*) She bore him a son, one of about twenty-five children.

ARCHER
(*Looks up at her and cries fervently*) Is she happy? I am worried about her happiness.

181

YEMUDEH

She often says there is no difference between her and a palace ornament. She doesn't elaborate. The controversy around her marriage has ceased to be news all over the world. Our parents shun talk about it. They sue whoever tries to revive the case. The Reed Dance continues unabated.

ARCHER

(*Crying with resignation*) O! Why did you come, Yemudeh? Why did you agree to be sent to remind me of her? Why has she become so heartless?

YEMUDEH

Shhhh, Archer. Shhhh. Many people in the world are in graceless marriages. An elder in the King's Council found her crying one day and told her that conflict, real and unreal, perpetuated the world. Don't cry yourself insane. Eventually she will be happy, but she wants you to forgive her first.

ARCHER

Was she told that I searched for her in mortuaries, morgues and sanatoria? Did anyone tell her I posted her photograph and missing-person flyers on every public notice board? Of her own volition she chose the King! O! How could I forgive her?

YEMUDEH

She wanted everyone to leave the palace alive. No love is deeper than that. Though you are thousands of miles away she feels the lump in your heart.

ARCHER

(*Rises and looks down at her. Calming*) Your voice and appearance are wrecking me. I can't believe I am talking to someone else. Could you please leave my room now, Yemudeh? (*Points at the exit*) I can't endure the agony.

YEMUDEH

(*Unzipping the bag*) Queen Mimudeh asked me to deliver this token to you. (*Exposing bundled wads of British pounds in the bag*) She says it's meant to assuage your heart.

ARCHER *stares at the bundles thunderstruck.*

(*Taking out the bundles one after the other and stacking them on a small space on the seat beside her hip*) Tradition stipulates such payment in goats and cows, but Her Highness thought you might require extra money in a cold country far from home. This is only £25 000; her way of saying bury the past and lumber on, Archer. She wishes you well and prays that you meet a suitable girlfriend. (*Drops the empty bag on the floor and stands up*) Tomorrow I am catching my return flight. A taxi is waiting for me downstairs. Goodbye, Archer. (*Saunters towards the door*)

ARCHER

(*Watches her tongue-tied and only regains speech when she touches the door handle*) Hey! (*Grabs the stack and hauls it her feet*) Take her money back! It was never about money! If she found justification in choosing the King, why is she sorry?

183

YEMUDEH

(*Frozen with her hand on the door handle, her back to him*) Do you really want to know?

ARCHER

Of course! Just tell me what's going on! Spit it out!

YEMUDEH

(*Demurs, but doesn't turn or leave the handle*) She is sorry about the unfortunate drama that happened at the end. It blew our scheme. (*Demurs again*) You met me first and sought my love. If your memory is good you'll recall that you spoke to me on Christmas Day. I was in the Third Form, you were in the Fifth. You told me people were not like coins —that if you lost me you wouldn't be able to find a replacement. I giggled and refused with my name. I didn't disclose to you that I had a twin. I loved you, but I was sceptical about dating. I then conspired with my twin before I left for a boarding school in January. She stepped into my shoes.

ARCHER

You mean Mimudeh was a caretaker lover?

YEMUDEH

(*Turning and looking at him*) She updated me religiously on your romantic progress —every word you said to her. She assured me she would surrender you to me when I was ready. Of course during school holidays you were strictly mine. I've all the photos and letters you wrote her.

ARCHER

I don't believe this is happening. Where is the evidence? Where are the photos?

YEMUDEH

Look in a side pocket in the bag. You'll also find her written confession on a certified affidavit.

ARCHER *bends, gropes inside the bag and draws a sheaf of handwritten letters and a cluster of photographs. He quickly shuffles the letters and photographs, some falling.*

In some of the photos you posed with my sister; in others with me. I always wore red and long sleeves when I was with you.

ARCHER

(*Gapes*) I – I don't know what to think, Yemudeh. My brain is stalling. Tell me about yourself. What then happened to you? (*Demurs*) Are you in a relationship?

YEMUDEH

I tattooed your initials on my forearm. (*Pulls back her right sleeves and shows him a tattoo:* **A-Mc**) I did it when I was in Form Three. Your initials are embossed on my radius and ulna. I'll take them to the grave.

ARCHER

(*Staring at her, the photos and letters trembling in his hands*) What's your occupation? (*Crossing to her slowly and dropping the letters and photos along the way*) Who is Yemudeh?

YEMUDEH

She is a final-year physiotherapy student at Cape Town University. After graduation she will join the Order of St Theresa and become a nun. Yemudeh will spend the rest of her life at an abbey rehabilitating the poor of India or Myanmar.

ARCHER *halts before her, shakes his head and holds her hands. She turns and looks away, but he pulls her to him and slides his hands around her waist, drawing her to him. Straining her head from him as if he is some contagious disease, she places her hands on his chest in a bid to push him away, but clutches the labels of his clothing and pulls him to her. Mourning moronically, they kiss recklessly.*

Final curtain

Afterword

The inspiring reports that gave birth to the foregoing play further stated that:

...under Swazi law, the monarch cannot be arrested or prosecuted. In court, angry discussions took place between traditionalists and modernists. Royalists argued that Miss Mahlangu had "fallen in love" with the king and was "deeply honoured" to be chosen. Rights activists said girls were being "raped" in the name of culture....

-The British Telegraph & BBC, October, 2002

... Mswati, who has ruled Swaziland – Africa's last absolute monarchy – since taking over from his father in 1986, celebrated his birthday this month with a $300 000 party, to which locals were encouraged to donate their own cattle for a feast.

With 13 wives and an estimated personal fortune of $100m, he is notorious for....

-Sunday Times (South Africa), 29 April, 2012

In its formative years and under a different title, a crude, experimental version amalgamating Book I and II was premiered at the Odyssey in the City of Kadoma, Zimbabwe, on 12th December, 2003. About a month later, it was performed at the Campbell Theatre in the same city, and subsequently at Jameson High School and many other secondary schools in the town for one year. The memorable premiering cast, to whom I am inexhaustibly indebted for according me those rare occasions when I saw in exactitude on stage what I had seen in my imagination, was as follows:

PERSONÆ	CHARACTER
George Yona	King Lima III
Tracey Ruth Machengo	Queen Amina
Sharon Zvidzai	Queen Liliosa
Abinail Chisango	Prof. Pitoni
Thomas Ferenando	Radimir Ivanov
Luke Mvura	PM Ete Gamato
Natasha Muhoni	Chuchu
Blessing Yotamu	Royal poet
Tafadzwa Makoni	Belemina
Samuel Phiri	MP Katomene
Sharon L. Mbano	Memudeh

As the playwright, director and producer, the full houses and standing ovations the production received spurred me into further research and script development, which culminated in *Squaring a Circle* and *Square Circle in a Triangle;* essentially an idealistic scholarship of ten years (2003 – 2013). However, work on this project was incessantly interrupted by other plays and novels I wrote during this period.

In conclusion, I also wish to express my tremendous indebtedness to Divine Fur, Managing Editor extraordinaire, for his belief in my literary abilities, and my gratitude to Dr Roselyn M. Jua, Senior Lecturer in American Literature at the University of Buea, Cameroon, whose meticulous and selfless editing of *The Lord of Anomy* primed me to write *The*

Shirburnian Catastrophe. And I would want to offer a heartfelt salute to Rosemary Ekosso, author of *The House of Falling Women*, who reviewed *Shrouded Blessings* and described it as "*a literary tour de force; a tantalising promise of more things to come*". The above individuals ignited in me the impetus to write, write and write.